Pause: Two Minutes to Tranquility

Discover Your Quiet Place Within

Patricia Boham, PhD

Pause: Two Minutes to Tranquility
By Patricia Boham, PhD

Published by: Nicasio Press,
                  Sebastopol, California
                  www.nicasiopress.com

ISBN: 979-8-9864100-7-4

Dedication

To all the stressed, busy people who think they don't have time to find the peace lurking beneath the constant thoughts that fill every waking moment.

ACKNOWLEDGEMENTS

I am most grateful for my husband and soulmate, Will Scofield. He believed in me, inspired me, and taught me so much. Though he died in 2019, I feel that wherever he is, he's saying, "See! I knew you could do it!"

I wish to thank Lee Lyon, teacher, friend, and cheerleader. He introduced me to the concept of the observer, and that helped me to change my relationship with my thoughts. It showed me the way to the quiet place inside.

When I began the book while living on Vancouver Island, I had never even considered writing a book and my only experience of a major writing project had been my doctoral dissertation. I am very grateful to Jeanette Taylor for her wisdom, guidance, and encouragement. She showed me how and convinced me that it was possible.

When I moved to Santa Fe, I was blessed to find Laura Duggan, editor and publisher, who has, with patience and wisdom, guided me the rest of the way.

Special thanks to Clare and Jack Radliffe and Pam Hyde for reading the final manuscript and for their valuable input. Thank you to Jack for suggesting the title, "Two Minutes to Tranquility," and to Pam for suggesting the subtitle, "Discover Your Quiet Place Within."

I sincerely appreciate my family and friends; they have been with me all the way through this eight-year project, and I couldn't have done it without them.

Cover Photos:

The photo on the front cover is of the confluence of the Oyster River and Woodhus Creek, which flowed past the author's home on Vancouver Island. If you look carefully, the red flecks in the photo are the salmon spawning. These beautiful natural waterways inspired Patricia and brought her much peace. She mentions them often in her book. The photo was taken by the author.

The photo on the back cover is the author and her dog, Amber, who provided inspiration and loving support through much of the writing process. They are sitting on a bench by the Oyster River at the edge of her property on Vancouver Island. This photo was taken by Michael DePledge.

Contents

Pause
Two Minutes to Tranquility

— *Time to Pause* —

I live in a world created by my thoughts
Until I Pause...
Notice my body and my breath
Feel the world of form beneath my feet
The air that gently brushes past my skin

Observe the thoughts and feelings
That drag around the past, bringing darkness into my day
Jump into the future pretending they can control
and predict it
Infuse it with worry and fear

As each breath moves through my body
I move deeper into my witness Self
This benevolent observer wraps my busy mind
in gratitude for its efforts
Smiles with loving compassion at the pain that's stored there

The image of the person I present to the world
Softens, emerges from behind old defenses
The peaceful place inside moves into my awareness
It's always there, just waiting for me to notice.

One breath at a time.
Living fully in the noisy world
I learn to mute the din within

INTRODUCTION

This book is designed to be like a cookbook. There are no complex theories to think about or time-consuming tasks to perform. *Pause* is a simple exercise designed to change the relationship you have with your thoughts and to bring you into a satisfying relationship with your quiet place inside.

Pause is designed to bring you into the present moment, allowing you to shift focus from the thoughts that would shape reality into what is really happening right now. It allows you to choose your responses to what life brings you without the complications of the old habits and beliefs in your head. With practice, it can be a pathway into mindfulness, where your attention is focused on the present moment. It can also serve as an introduction to meditation if you have more time to spend on it.

The *Pause* exercise is simple and can be done in less than a minute. It is designed to work for everyone who feels they don't have time to meditate. For meditators, it brings the benefits of meditation into the present moment. It is not complicated and can be done in the course of a few conscious breaths. It just requires practice so that it is available to apply to life, whether on the run or at home in your favourite chair.

The first few chapters describe the practice and teach you how to *Pause*. The remaining chapters provide an opportunity to apply *Pause* to your own life. You will be able to pick and choose what applies to you. After you learn how to *Pause*, you can read the chapters in any order that appeals to you.

For this practice to have an impact on your life, take time to read and do the exercises labeled "Try this." You may even want to give yourself time to try an exercise for a few days before returning to the book and working with another. In this way, your experience will grow organically.

For some, *Pause* will evolve into a spiritual experience, but for many, it will simply be a pathway to mindfulness and a practical tool with which to quiet the incessant thoughts in their heads.

Several years ago, I began to write blank verse in my journal rather than the usual journal entries about what was happening from day to day. When I *paused* and my mind became quiet, words would seem to percolate up from the quiet place inside of me and express my true experience of the moment. I included some of these verses and unless otherwise noted, I wrote the poetry you will encounter in these pages.

I sincerely hope this book helps you to change the relationship you have with your thoughts and brings to you a deeply satisfying relationship with your quiet place inside. It is there waiting to welcome you home.

PART I – THE BASICS

PAUSE:
Practice Awareness Until Stillness Ensues

When I learned to *Pause*, it changed my life. It helped me to find peace and equanimity during a very challenging time. It continues to sustain me through the grief of losing my husband, Will, and daughter, Erin, within two years of each other

In 2015, my husband became ill, and I cared for him at home until he died in January of 2019. Prior to his illness, we had been retired for ten years. We were both clinical psychologists and for many years had been reading, listening, searching spiritual and psychological paths to find that elusive, peaceful place inside.

When I became his full-time caregiver, I suddenly found that I had no time for my long meditations, and for about the first three months, I was in overwhelm. I lost the equanimity and peace I had found through meditation, yet I needed it more than ever.

Meditation had given me a shift in focus: *out* of the constant thoughts that bombard most of us, and *into* a quiet place. I remembered something that I had used and taught clients over the years when my life was busy. Herbert Benson had called it the "Relaxation Response" and Charles Stroebel had referred to the "Quieting Reflex." Both were designed to alleviate stress in people with busy lives, who may or may not have even wanted to learn to meditate. I took the concept and applied what I learned from meditation practice and called it *Pause,* an acronym for "Practice Awareness Until Stillness Ensues."

I also called it *Pause* because my life reminded me of a nonstop video, and the first conscious breath reminded me of the pause icon on a video.

HOW TO PAUSE:

1. Take a deep breath, and as you exhale, let the breath move through your body taking tension with it.
2. Observe your body, and if it is still tense, allow a few more exhales to take the tension with them. If the tension persists, don't fight it, just observe it, and move on to the next step.
3. Now step back, as if from a distance, and observe your thoughts and feelings. Don't judge them or try to force them to stop. Just observe them as if they are the dialogue in a play, and you are in the audience.

YOUR QUIET PLACE INSIDE

It is from a peaceful mind that a peaceful perception of the world is experienced.

Gerald Jampolsky

Humans have been trying to describe this quiet place since the beginning of recorded history. It's mysterious because our minds have to get out of the way in order for us to feel it, and therefore it's hard to find words to express the experience. Many religions try to grapple with it and in the process often move it out of the reach of their flock with rules for getting there and even making it the purview of only the priests, saints, and gurus. This phenomenon is part of what motivated me to write this book.

When I was a teenager, I went to church mainly to hear the benediction at the end of the service: "May the peace that passes all understanding be with you." My busy teenage mind wanted relief from all its worries and fears. I wanted that peace inside.

I have continued the search for that elusive peace to this day and when I discovered *Pause*, I realized that I might be getting close to finding it. I have learned that what disturbs the peace inside of me often has less to do with the situation at hand than what I am telling myself about it. My constant conditioned thoughts create most of the turmoil that drowns out the peace inside of me.

I have a favourite image of the quiet space inside: I imagine a pond or lake. The surface can be disturbed by storms, wind, rain, or hail, yet deep within, the water is calm and undisturbed. I often use this when I begin a meditation, or I just *Pause* and shift my focus to this image when the going gets rough during the day.

I have been sharing *Pause* for a long time and leading meditation groups where people *Pause* for day-by-day, moment-to-moment mindfulness, or as part of their meditation. I have not experienced anyone who has not been able to find quiet under their incessant thoughts, if they practice.

When you create distance from the thoughts that roll around in your head, they lose their credibility and ability to define your reality. Observing your thoughts changes your perspective and the impact they have on our experience of the present moment. A conscious breath acts like the pause button on the otherwise nonstop video of our lives.

These tools begin our journey inward to the quiet place inside. On this journey we can experience everything from a momentary relief from a negative thought all the way to a profound experience of deep peace…practice is our ticket to ride on this journey.

TRY THIS:

1. Find an image that brings a sense of peace to you. This is often a place in nature, but experiment until you find what works best for you.
2. Pause and notice how you feel more peaceful as you stop listening to and believing all your thoughts.
3. Tell yourself this quiet place is always inside, just waiting for you to notice.
4. Go to this place often so that it is readily available when you need it.

YOUR OBSERVER

As soon as I become conscious of my breath, my observer or witness is engaged. I am capable of observing my breathing, my body, my feelings, and my thoughts. I am also able to show up in the present moment, paying attention to the world around me instead of being distracted by the thoughts going around and around in my head.

We could say that our observer is our conduit into mindfulness. It is the road that leads to the quiet place inside from which we can access all the treasures therein. This road is paved with perspective. Unless we stand back and observe our thoughts objectively, we just go along listening to them and believing them. The observer makes it possible to shift our awareness from our thoughts to the quiet place inside. In that wise place, we know that we are not our thoughts.

With practice we may even begin to recognize habitual responses and be able to understand where they came from. For example, I am afraid of snakes, even when they are not dangerous, because I picked up on my mother's fear of garter snakes in our garden.

When I observe where my reactions come from, I realize I am not my fear, my anger, and my impatience. When those emotions come up, *Pause* puts them in their place. I understand them as remnants of the past that my mind still applies to the present. When I observe them with compassion, it is such a relief to know that in the present moment, I have a choice. I can either go along with old conditioned thoughts or show up clear and calmly ready to respond to the world from my quiet place. This also allows me to deal with real danger or real situations that would elicit fear or anger, with integrity, rather than just reacting and regretting later how I handled the situation.

The better we understand where our reactions come from, the easier it is to recognize that they are caused by thoughts and not who we really are. We have a choice. We can act rather than react.

TRY THIS:

1. *Pause* and observe your surroundings. Are you aware of what you are seeing, hearing, feeling, smelling, touching, or are you "lost in thought?"
2. While you are eating, *Pause*, observe where your thoughts are. Now notice the taste of food in your mouth.
3. *Pause* and observe your thoughts, even briefly, when you are with other people. Are you paying attention to them or to what your thoughts are telling you about them?
4. As you go about your day, *Pause* often and just observe your thoughts objectively.

MAKING *PAUSE* AUTOMATIC

Pause is simple. It can be done as you go about your busy day. When you stop for a red light in traffic, you can *Pause* rather than fret over having to stop. When you are on hold on the phone, *Pause*; in the bathroom, *Pause*. Make use of the natural pauses in the momentum of your days to shift your awareness from how your thoughts and feelings are interpreting reality.

I have found that interpreting life though the quiet place inside rather than though the conditioned thoughts in my head has been life-changing for me.

You don't have to set aside time to *Pause*, but practice transforms it from an idea in your head to an automatic response to life. When I have time, or set aside time, I stay with the quiet place and turn it into a meditation. Throughout the meditation, when thoughts and feelings barge in, I observe them with compassion, and if they are important, I sometimes promise to deal with them when I finish my meditation. I am in charge now; my thoughts are not.

There is a simple gimmick that can help *Pause* become automatic. Get some file-folder dots and put them in places that you see frequently, like on your watch, phone, computer, bathroom door, kitchen door, and so forth. Every time you see one of your dots, *Pause*.

TRY IT AGAIN BEFORE YOU MOVE ON:

1. Take a deep breath, and as you exhale, let the breath move through your body taking tension with it.
2. Observe your body, and if it is still tense, allow a few more exhales to take the tension with them. If the tension persists, don't fight it, just observe it, and move on to the next step.
3. Now observe your thoughts and feelings. Don't judge them or try to force them to stop. Just observe them as if they are the dialogue in a play, and you are in the audience.
4. Integrate this into your life by taking time to *Pause* whenever you catch a negative thought or emotion, or when you are waiting at a stoplight or on hold on the phone or in line at the grocery store.

WHEN YOUR BODY DOESN'T GIVE UP ITS TENSION

My body's convinced
Danger's still there
Hangs on tight
While I Pause

Our bodies have been accustomed to tensing up in response not only to real threats from outside but also from the danger our thoughts concoct for us in the course of our days. We need to appreciate how our minds and bodies protect us from real danger and learn to recognize when our thoughts are creating a false alarm. The fight/flight hormones tense our bodies when we truly confront the sabre-toothed tiger and when our thoughts make up a saber-toothed tiger.

No matter how your body responds when you are allowing your breath to move through it, don't fight it. Observe your body: Is there a particular part that is holding tension? If that is the case, breathe into that tight place. If you have more time, allow more breaths to move through it; imagine that the breaths are taking tension with them.

If your body just tenaciously holds on, smile, and move on to observing your thoughts and feelings. They will often explain why your body doesn't want to let go.

In the beginning it may be harder to release tension. Like learning any exercise, practice helps. If you shift your focus to your body as you breathe, it will help you come into awareness of not only your body but also the present moment. Whether you are paying attention to it or not, your body is aware of your surroundings, smells the flowers, hears a bird singing, feels the air on your skin.

When we *Pause*, we are forming a new relationship with our bodies, a conscious one. Rather than rushing about, taking them for granted, we become aware of our body with newfound appreciation each time we *Pause*.

TRY THIS:

1. When you have a few extra minutes, treat your body to a time when it has your full attention. Take a deep breath, and as you exhale, observe what it really feels like in all of its nooks and crannies.
2. Be like a parent who has been too busy to stop and focus on a child; really listen and appreciate this amazing machine we live in and usually take for granted.
3. Respond to any complaints with a nurturing breath and a smile.
4. Your body might ask you to move into a more comfortable position, stretch, or change your posture.
5. Try tensing and relaxing from head to toe. Breathe into tight spots.
6. Smile and appreciate your home in this lifetime— your body.

WHEN YOUR THOUGHTS JUST WON'T BE QUIET

Shall I live this day inside my head
Filled with demons of my own devising?

Only once in all the years that I have been sharing *Pause* have I met someone who was immediately able to calm her thoughts. If you are having difficulty getting your mind to stop pushing the present moment out of the way while it tries to control the future, rehash the past, judge, worry, and argue, you are normal.

My mind has an opinion about everything, set ideas about the best way to do things. It has been working hard to keep me safe all my life and in the process, it has become like an authority who knows all about me and has an opinion about what I should do in every situation. All this is based on old beliefs and experiences and is not guided by the reality of the present moment. My mind actually manufactures its own reality. If it were another person sitting next to me and talking nonstop, I would have moved out of range a long time ago.

I sometimes think my mind is like a small child. If left unattended, it just goes about dismantling the house, creating a mess that I will have to clean up. It isn't malicious; it just doesn't function without supervision. When I press the pause button and observe my thoughts, I am the supervisor guiding my mind back where it belongs, into the moment. The mind is a useful tool, filled with skills for daily living. I appreciate how hard it works and won't fight with it; I smile with compassion as I observe it. In the stillness present when my thoughts are not in charge, there is wisdom, intuition, and compassion, which can guide me to function in this lifetime.

TRY THIS:

1. Observe your thoughts; see them as a nonstop video, and push the pause button with a breath.
2. Keep pressing the pause button on the video your thoughts are creating until you begin to achieve a sense of mastery that will become stronger with practice.
3. Watch your thoughts with appreciation, compassion, and a smile.
4. Don't fight your thoughts. They will win because if we are fighting them, we are using thoughts to battle thoughts, and they are still in charge.

LIFE IS A PLAY

Shakespeare called the world a stage
My life upon that stage
Needs a new director.

As I continue to *Pause* and shift my focus from the automatic thoughts that would run through my head 24/7, I notice how much power I have given those thoughts to direct my life. They are the product of my ego and are based on everything I have learned and experienced throughout my lifetime. They very often do not reflect what is really happening in the moment.

When I *Pause,* I move into the audience and observe my life on the stage. Here is what I find—there are three major contributors to my play:

My ego, which is really my conditioned mind, provides most of the dialogue in my play. She is pretty pushy. As a wannabe director, she repeats old scripts based on past learning and experience that often don't relate to the present. She relies on old beliefs that limit the possibilities for scripts with more positive outcomes because of her old fears and limitations. She does, however, have some useful information and experience and an important role to play as the resident librarian.

My observer is the one with the right qualifications to be the director. She is capable of standing back and evaluating the ceaseless thought dialogue in light of what is really happening in the moment. She lives in the present moment and interprets a script based on what is happening now rather than the past and future. She can observe but does not become emotionally attached to the fears, beliefs, and reactions spewing forth from my ego.

Under the observer's direction, the set becomes quiet, the setting is the present moment, and all players can be heard.

My quiet wise Self is the heroine. She waits patiently in the wings, sometimes for years, until she can be heard beyond the mind-made din of my thoughts. She is often glimpsed when she provides intuition, though even then, she is often ignored. Self is calm, loving, and compassionate. Even if an angry ogre pushes onto the set or a storm rages, Self meets all with quiet wisdom, free of the preconceived ideas that ego would bring to the scene. She is not passive; she comes up with solutions that work better than ones based on old information. She is free to see situations as they really are in the moment. She doesn't carry the old baggage from which blame, vindictiveness and helplessness come from. This Self doesn't do drama; she is more like a wise, compassionate actress doing improvisation in the present moment.

No matter where the play seems to be going and how much drama arrives on the stage, a moment to *Pause* can give the observer the director's chair, move ego to a supporting role, and allow Self to handle the scene with grace.

TRY THIS:

1. Imagine that your life is a play on YouTube, a video about some drama in your life.
2. Stand back and observe the drama, then click pause.
3. Observe the thoughts and belief systems that are writing the script for your play.
4. Continue to *Pause* until your quiet Self is able to create calm and clarity in the scene.

HAPPINESS IS AN INSIDE JOB

There is nothing good or bad,
but thinking makes it so.   —*Shakespeare*

One morning, while living in the woods by the river on Vancouver Island, I woke up with my head fussing about my life. My mood had moved in to support the efforts of my ego to make my life into some kind of image it thought I should have and didn't believe I could have. I was feeling fearful and discouraged.

I began my yoga with a moment to *Pause* and stood back from my thoughts with my observer. I observed my thoughts about what my life should be and the fears about what could happen. The act of observing these thoughts allowed me to see them objectively, and the feelings that had been attached to them subsided and allowed me to show up in the moment. When my focus shifted, I saw the beauty of the woods and river for the first time that day, though it had been waiting for me to notice ever since I opened my eyes. I was filled by a sense of quiet joy. I was happy.

What happens in my life has less impact on my happiness than what I think about what is happening. Happiness is largely an inside job, and so is unhappiness.

Nothing about my life had changed. I still don't know what will happen next. I have no way of knowing what is ahead for me as I age. I'm new at it! I only know that as soon as my thoughts ceded the floor to the experience of being in the moment, I was happy.

My New Year's resolution has been to deepen my awareness that happiness comes from not needing my world to be different than it is. That happens when I am not listening to the regrets and dire predictions my mind creates to take the place of reality. Sometimes reality is rough. But when we don't fight it and instead deal with it without telling ourselves "it isn't fair," we can show up and deal with it constructively.

My thoughts also seem to specialize in making judgments...about almost everything. The judgments most often seem to be negative, like "it's not supposed to be raining today." If I just listen obediently to that thought, I am not happy because it is raining. When I lived in a rain forest, I had lots of opportunity to practice with that one. The unhappiness about the rain was coming from my mind telling me what I couldn't do because it's raining and often said, "woe is me" about how often it rains. When I sit back, breathe, and observe, pretty soon, my thoughts are quieter. I notice the shining beauty of the wet leaves, the colour of the moss, a bird enjoying a puddle, and I feel a peaceful sense of contentment with the moment just as it is: it's raining today.

TRY THIS:

1. Think about something in your life that is interfering with your happiness. Observe it objectively.
2. If there is something you can do to change it, get constructive with your solution.
3. Question and try to change thoughts you have that are making the situation worse, like shame and blame.
4. Whenever you are unhappy, take a breath, observe your feelings and thoughts as if you were a loving compassionate friend. Notice how much of your distress is being created by your thoughts.

Finding Patterns

The automatic thoughts that run through my head carry so many detriments to my happiness. As I observed them recently, I realized that they tell me about severe limitations to possibilities and potential in my life. It is impossible to know all that the future holds, but if I listen to my thoughts, they are full of dire predictions about what my life as widow might hold. When I stand back and look at those predictions, they don't match the experience of my life in this moment. Yet that is all any of us has, one moment at a time. I might just as well enjoy those moments as they come.

When problems do arise, if I deal with them without listening to the drama my conditioned mind would make of the situation, I hear the intuitive wisdom that resides in my quiet place. When problems arise, I want to be able to do my best to cope with them while not needing life to be different before I can be at peace and even happy.

Most of us have a well-worn litany of favourite negative messages that we apply to life as it unfolds. As I continue to listen to mine from an objective point-of-view, as if they belonged to someone else, I see some patterns. If I spend some time observing them, I can often see where they came from. Sometimes I can almost hear my mother's voice telling me I should be doing something more useful, or my Grade One teacher, at the new school I transferred into in the middle of the term, telling me I was behind, so I thought I wasn't as smart as the other kids. Even a PhD hasn't shut that one up! Our minds have difficulty changing beliefs that we pick up over the years, especially when the message was delivered at a vulnerable time in our lives.

Practice helps. As time goes on and I notice what my thoughts are telling me when I *Pause*, I have begun to recognize patterns and recurrent negative messages. The repetitions help me to more clearly see that they are from the past and not relevant to what is going on in the moment.

TRY THIS:

1. When you *Pause* and catch a thought, notice it and say, out loud to yourself, if you are alone, "Oh, there is the message about doing something more useful. Thanks, Mom." If you are not alone, make a mental note.
2. If you really want to interrupt the repetitive messages, write them down. When you see them on the page, it is even easier to question their validity.
3. Sometimes there are also positive messages, like "My father told me I could do anything I set my mind to." I keep that one, and this process even helps me to remember it when it would come in handy.

CHOOSE YOUR MOOD

My mood
Obeys my mind

My mind
Supports my mood

Together they hide
The peaceful place inside

Moods are mostly an inside job. They can also be triggered by an outside event, but even then, negative reactions to that event are very often caused by the way our minds interpret what has happened.

As I continue to remember to *Pause,* I am amazed at what I am discovering about my moods. I observe whatever mood is present; pausing and naming it takes the sting out of grumpy, sad, mad, helplessness, hopelessness, jealousy, and all their friends and associates. When I am able to move into my observer self and objectively listen to my moods, I most often find that they are not in sync with what is really happening in the moment. They are most often a result of what my mind is feeding me.

I am also finding that many of my moods fall into patterns. They respond to familiar litanies of thoughts and at almost predictable times of day and in similar situations.

With this discovery, I decided to do a mood check when I first get out of bed in the morning. I have formed the habit of taking time to *Pause* as my feet hit the floor, rather than just beginning the day with whatever my mind is producing. Since most often, nothing has had a chance to happen yet, it is easier to see that the mood was produced by the thoughts that pushed in as soon as I became conscious. I then have a choice about how I want to feel. I can choose to see this as a new day with the potential to make it a good one.

Years ago, I found an idea in the *New Yorker* magazine for beginning the day and I have been using it for a long time—telling myself, "Please God, get into my head before I do!" when I first wake up.

As the day unfolds, many thoughts and moods come and go, dancing though my awareness, hiding the reality of life. I found a quote by Evelyn Underhill: "For lack of attention, a thousand forms of loveliness elude us every day." As each mood unfolds, notice how familiar it is. Many of them have been around for a long time. Taking the time to *Pause* breaks the hold of thoughts and moods.

TRY THIS:

1. *Pause.* Observe your mood and write about it.
2. Describe the thoughts that are supporting the mood.
3. Observe the thoughts that instigated the mood.
4. Notice when a mood instigates more thoughts to support that mood.
5. Write your observations in a notebook and read back through it from time to time.

REPARENTING YOURSELF

No matter what happens
I have a thought about it.

It is based on a guidebook
I have been writing all my life.

Stop reading for a few minutes and tell me your life story. Were you welcomed into this world by parents who loved you right from your first breath? Or did you land in the lap of a parent or parents who were distraught by life and you were one more problem for them to cope with? Did they praise you and take pride in you, or could you never figure out how to please them? All these factors and many more contribute to your thoughts for the rest of your life.

When you have a job to do, what you were taught about your competence as a child probably influences your level of confidence in your abilities now. How you perceived the way your family felt about you colours your relationships now. Your feeling of self-worth may still reflect the degree of approval you received as a child.

I have a friend who was born in Europe at the beginning of WWII. The family already had four boys, and he was supposed to be a girl. His arrival was greeted by a groan. His mother never welcomed him; his brothers suggested they send him back. As the youngest, he was never able to compete with his brothers. At age eight, he was further ostracized by being sent to a boarding school where he didn't even speak the language. Today, he is a lovely man, but the unloved child who believed he could never measure up is often the author of his thoughts.

When we *Pause* and observe our thoughts objectively, with some practice, we can begin to recognize that they don't make sense in terms of what's really happening in the moment. If we fight with those thoughts, we can't win, so we need to just observe them. Many of those thoughts are the voice of the child we once were. That child was vulnerable, often scared and just trying to figure out how to navigate this big scary world.

If I stand back in my observer and really look at the child I once was, I would feel love and compassion for her. I would realize how hard she tried to just cope. I would want to take her in my arms and hold her and tell her how much I appreciate what she tried to do.

My observer allows me to focus on my wise Self, and the child inside of me can learn to trust that wise adult Self, who is better than any parent I might have wished for. That Self is "in house," always available when I need her. In her warm embrace, fearful thoughts become quiet, and the past is no longer in control of the present moment. With my observer, I have a new way of interpreting the present moment, unrelated to old fears and experiences. I have access to the clear perspective of my quiet place. Loving compassionate wisdom is always as near as a *Pause*, a breath, and an observation of the moment.

It takes practice to change a deeply ingrained belief system that originated in childhood and has been added to by experiences along the way. It is the squirrel in the wheel that goes around and around in our heads incessantly. We have been listening and believing, and it has moved in and replaced a great deal of the reality in each moment.

It's time to replace the parents in your head with the adult Self who lives inside of you and who always has your back. It's time to change your relationship with messages from your automatic thoughts. When they come up, you can recognize that many of them began with a precious, courageous kid, and you can love and appreciate him or her, rather than criticize and doubt yourself.

If you can do this following exercise, you are on the way to reparenting yourself. When you stand back and observe your thoughts, you will be able to do so with increasing compassion…the battle with your mind is on the way to a truce. This is an important step on the road to inner harmony where your thoughts and wise intuition can work together.

TRY THIS:

1. Take a self-limiting or negative thought that arises frequently for you as you observe your thoughts. Remember significant times in your life that it has appeared.
2. Follow the thought back as far as you can. For example, you might say, "Last week at work, I doubted that I could handle the project I was given, even though I have successfully done something similar before." This might go all the way back to your reaction when your older sister could tie her shoes and you couldn't.
3. Stand back and observe the way your self-doubts grew over the years. Focus on the child you once were, trying to tie your shoelaces. You were too young to be able to do it, but you didn't know that at the time.
4. Now imagine yourself as you are today, being able to go back and reassure your young self that when you are a little older you will be very able to tie your shoes, and in the meantime, you love the way you tried. As a matter of fact, you see the beginnings of the strong person you have become. In spite of old fears, you jump in and try and usually succeed.

THE *PAUSE* PERSPECTIVE

World order crumbling?
Sound bites of news,
Energy of fear,
Assault me.

With a Pause,
Perspective
Adds compassion,
Not fear to the fray

The day that the US Capitol was attacked by a mob, sending shock waves around the world, I made the mistake of watching too much news. The pundits were pounding their words into my consciousness; my body and mind felt the energy of fear moving through me like a current of electricity. I turned off the TV and still felt the sound waves affecting my nervous system. I didn't sleep well for two nights, and it didn't let up when I closed my eyes and ears.

I realized I had had enough! I took time to *Pause* and found perspective.

I breathed, observed my body, and noticed my nervous system seemed wired into the collective fear of violence, of the breakdown of a system that we count on to keep us safe. I sent a lot of conscious breaths through my body until it began to relax. As my body began to respond, I noticed the trees and the silence, filled only with the sound of the river. It was then easier to observe my thoughts. They were still whirling in the chaos of events and the world's reaction to them. They were so firmly caught up in the storm that I needed to send some new thoughts to help my mind come back into the moment.

This is a place where imagery can sometimes help. As I shared earlier, I have a favourite and am glad I have practiced so that it's ready when I need it. I imagine a lake. Under the surface there is a deep calm place. On the surface the storm is raging and waves are crashing. I take my imagination to the deep quiet under the surface and allow that stillness to fill me.

I don't want to be like an ostrich with my head in the sand. I want to be aware of what is happening in the real world, in the moment, and even help if I can. My best chance of being helpful is when I'm not so caught up in my emotions that I lose access to the quiet intuitive place inside where I am most apt to find the wisdom to help constructively.

As I practiced all that I am suggesting, my body felt less wired. My fight-or-flight response was no longer bathing my organs in hormones released by stress. A feeling of quiet strength replaced the helplessness of watching the attack on the structure of a system that I have been blessed to live in. So many people in the world have lived through wars and upheaval and not had the luxury of security I have taken for granted. When it felt threatened, I wanted to lovingly tend it. If I had gone into anger at those who encouraged and those who stormed the capitol, I would have become part of that storm. I want to live with perspective and understand the fear and pain that convinces people that the only option is violence.

I think helplessness that showed up as anger may have been causing my reaction. I recognize how easy it would be to allow the righteous indignation I felt to fuel a matching anger in me. Anger on one side pitted against anger on the other could keep this storm brewing for years. I don't want to contribute to that scenario, so I am going to *Pause* as often as it takes to find that wise Self inside me that has something else to contribute.

Becoming objective gives you the power and energy to find constructive solutions, even if initially you fear that objectivity is complacence or acceptance. It is just the opposite.

TRY THIS:

1. Think about something that makes you angry or afraid…and *Pause*.
2. Breathe and observe until you are able to see the situation objectively. It may take some practice to get to an objective place. I'm not suggesting that you accept it as okay, but just that you bring objective clarity to it.
3. When you reach an objective place, there will be a sense of calm you might never have experienced about this issue. That calm place allows access to your wise Self and the intuitive constructive approaches that can eventually free you from the pain of helplessness and anger.
4. From that objective place, if there is something that you want to do about it, you will be more effective.

— *Time to Pause* —

I am the observer of
All aspects of my identity in this lifetime
Mother, wife, lover, friend, psychologist, teacher, writer...
When I die all of those will be gone.

As I observe that truth
I feel freedom
Loving compassion
For all the work I have done
To create and hang onto
That which will be gone
With my last breath

Every time I Pause
Move into my observer
Free from thoughts
I am beyond time
Beyond attachment to my identity
I am in a place of love, free from judgment and fear

WHAT THE PRESENT MOMENT FEELS LIKE

Problems
Insurmountable
In my head
Fade to
Insignificance
In my soul

One morning as I began my yoga, I felt weighted down by problems. There were issues playing over and over in my head like videos stuck on a loop, or about three loops. Rather than just letting my head have its way and spoil my yoga time, I stood still, looked out at the forest, took some time to *Pause*, and examined each problem as if it were playing on a video. The objectivity released the emotional charge that had been attached to the incessant repetition of woes. Love and compassion flowed from my centre, filled my awareness. Such relief!

After yoga, my dog Amber and I went for a walk and damned if the loops of problems didn't start up again! So I did it again. I paused the video loops in my head and because practice helps, the sense of calm came back faster this time. With the freedom from incessant thoughts came an intense awareness of the beauty of nature all around me. The cedars and firs were flocked with remnants of the first snowfall, but my mind was so quiet, it didn't even describe the scene at that moment. There was no separation between me and the world around me. I was filled with love.

Moments like this are reality. We experience what is real in the moment when our minds are quiet, when they are not drowning out the experience of the moment.

Sometimes when spiritual or religious teachers describe the disappearance of personal boundaries and the merging with all that is—oneness, awakening—it seems that they are describing something that only happens to gurus and saints. I so often hear, "If you can describe it, it isn't the real thing." I have always resisted that approach. I think something that feels this good should be available to everyone. I believe we are all capable of finding it if we can just learn to quiet our minds. When our minds are quiet, we are in the moment, and we know oneness because our thoughts aren't separating us.

I had a teacher who called these experiences epiphanies and was the first person to suggest to me that this is reality. He suggested paying attention to moments like this, making a note, remembering them. Most of us just let them pass because they are difficult to describe in words, and our culture hasn't described them as part of the experience of ordinary people like me. Using *Pause* on a regular basis and learning to quiet your mind, your epiphanies will become more frequent and more real.

TRY THIS:

1. For the next week pay attention to your epiphanies. Don't shrug them off as a fluke. The moment when you see a sunset, your thoughts stop, and you are one with it is real. If you see a child, an animal, or a flower and feel a sudden rush of love and oneness, that's real.
2. Write down all your epiphanies and come back to them in moments of stress.
3. Look in your past for epiphanies. What did you learn, and how did they change you?

PAUSE FOR LOVING-KINDNESS

My lovely old dog
On her special blanket on the couch
Follows me with her eyes as I move about

I look into her adoring eyes
My heart pops open
Love pours from the depths of my being

For thirteen years she has been teaching me
Loving-Kindness

I think dogs are gifted teachers of loving-kindness; they just love without judgment no matter what we do.

I read Jack Kornfield's book *The Wise Heart*, and in the last chapter he urges the reader to develop the practice of the Buddhist Four Limitless Qualities: loving-kindness, compassion, joy, and peace. In this practice, we are urged to direct each of these qualities, beginning with loving-kindness, toward ourselves first, then toward someone we love, then moving out to friends, family, strangers, and even our enemies.

When I tried to see even loved ones, and most difficult, myself, in a loving, compassionate non-judgment way, I couldn't just flow into the feelings the way I sensed Amber did.

I stopped trying to force myself to do the exercise and had myself *Pause* instead. When my observer came out and looked at the thoughts that were pouring over my attempt to do the exercise, I was shocked. I saw that my mind was circling the wagons of judgment around me. To one degree or another, it was protecting me from even the loveliest people. It was showing me every possible way that they could hurt me.

I sat with this realization, continued to breathe, relaxed my body, and allowed my mind to throw up every judgment and fear about each person I tried to focus on. As I gained increased perspective of what my mind was doing, my defenses began to fade.

As my mind became calmer, I began to feel the loving-kindness and compassion from deep inside flow out to everyone I brought in for the exercise. In the space that *Pause* provided for me to observe my thoughts and stop believing them, love and compassion for my own mind soothed and reassured it. The armour fell away, and I could feel love. A gentle feeling of peace and a quiet joy ensued and included everyone and everything I brought into my focus.

Our egos try to separate us from other people and the world around us, believing that everything is a threat. I find that *Pause* gives me the opportunity to stop believing the ego's primary messages of fear. When I am not focused on and believing fear, the natural well of love and compassion that lives in the quiet place under my thoughts comes into focus and makes love possible.

I am aware that whenever I saw the directions for loving-kindness practice, I would try it, but not stay with it. I was practicing it in my head, where all the barriers to loving-kindness live. As I continued to *Pause*, it helped to pave the way for the breakthrough I feel today.

I feel closer to understanding the great teacher of loving-kindness, the Dalai Lama. I am not there yet, but I now understand what he has been trying to teach me, along with Thich Nhat Hahn, Pema Chödrön, and other gifted teachers. They are teaching practice! Developing the habit of pouring loving-kindness and compassion on myself and others, so it is the norm. Observe judgment rather than believing it.

I am grateful for my commitment to *Pause*, as it has enabled me to combine it with loving-kindness practice and feel the gradual shift from a life of judgmental thinking to a life of mindful, compassionate interactions with the world. Joy and peace follow naturally for me when I love without reserve, and I am safer than my mind would ever have been able to imagine.

TRY THIS:

1. *Pause*, breathe, and observe your body and your surroundings.

2. Bring your attention to something that is easy to love —an animal, a flower, a tree, or a bird. Observe whatever your thoughts are saying about it.

3. Soften your focus and as you observe your thoughts about it objectively, allow yourself to be aware of its beauty, the magic of the life energy in it.

4. If you find yourself softening toward it, beginning to let it in and love it, just sit with that feeling.

5. If you find it difficult to let your defenses down and the love to flow, don't criticize yourself for that. Thank your ego for working so hard to protect you and tell your conditioned thoughts that it's safe to love this animal, flower or whatever you have chosen. Again, just sit with it.

6. No matter how this exercise works for you when you first do it, congratulate yourself for what you are doing and allow yourself to move on, knowing that every time you come back and practice this exercise, it will get easier.

7. At some point, you will be ready to try it with a person. Start with a person who is easiest for you to love and work with that in the same way.

8. The last and most difficult focus for this exercise is yourself. Again, follow the same steps.

MY MIND'S FAVOURITE ISSUE

Thoughts and feelings
Like a gerbil on a wheel
Until I Pause
Observe the gerbil isn't real.

Research has shown that our thoughts chew on the same issues year after year. The more I *Pause* and observe my thoughts, the more I am aware of what my conditioned mind most likes to dwell on. When I look back, I have to agree with the research—the basic issues are the same, only names and faces have changed.

I have known people who are fixated on being perfect, on never making a mistake, on being victims, on martyrdom, guilt, being the biggest and the best, and on and on. If you continue to *Pause* and observe your thoughts, you will find your main themes.

My main theme is the need to be liked. If I think someone is mad at me or if I think I did something to annoy someone, when I *Pause* and observe my thoughts, I hear my mind creating negative scenarios with people who would likely be surprised by the dramas that I have created in my head. These thoughts can intrude on the enjoyment of a beautiful day, even precious time with a loved one. They are pushy and demand attention. There are times when I have to *Pause* several times before they subside and fade into the background so I can experience the calm in my centre.

When I stop listening to my thoughts, I often realize that the angry dialogue in my head was not based on anything anyone had actually said or done. I am capable of making the whole thing up using even a tiny thread of unrelated information. I remember the essence of Robert Burns' poem. He suggested that if we knew how often people think of us, we wouldn't be so worried about what they think.

I often use the example of walking down the street and seeing an old friend coming toward me. I say "hello." They don't respond and keep on walking. If I let my conditioned thoughts attach meaning to that event, they will bedevil me with stories about how the person is angry with me, doesn't like me, has told everyone I am a bad person, and so on. If I keep encouraging it by listening to all that, it can get pretty convincing, all in the absence of any real information. My conditioned thoughts seldom offer up the possibility that the person was preoccupied and hadn't even seen or recognized me. The quiet wise place inside, under the thoughts, will readily allow for more reasonable and less negative possibilities. From there, I can just decide to give the person a call and check it out...or not.

TRY THIS:

1. For one day, but preferably a week, every time you *Pause* and observe your thoughts, note the theme. If you write down the theme, it will be even easier to identify your chosen preoccupations!
2. When you identify your theme, notice how it impacts your life—when it intrudes on a present moment and pushes aside something you would have enjoyed.
3. Notice when you are listening to an argument or a raft of accusations coming from inside your head, and smile.

THE IMPERFECT SELF

Any journey into the past
Will follow a pathway strewn with mistakes
Greet each imperfection with gratitude
Lesson learned

Observe with compassion
Move forward to the present
Knowing each step into the future
Is a new opportunity

Memories of mistakes are constant fodder for my thoughts. I often wonder how my ego can feel so helpless, unfairly judged, and inadequate, while at the same time it feels so much responsibility, for even big things that go wrong. I sometimes call that phenomenon "helpless omnipotence."

Thoughts of "should'a, could'a, would'a" take up a lot of space in the incessant thoughts that whirl around if unchecked. They colour some of our most difficult memories, like the death of a loved one, the loss of a job, or a friendship. These losses are hard enough without beating ourselves up for not, somehow, being able to change what happened. For example, I've yet to meet a parent, including myself, who doesn't feel guilty for not having been able to prevent some pain in the lives of their children.

Standing back and observing what you tell yourself about the mistakes you feel you made will give you a clearer perspective and allow you to apologize or make amends if that is called for, and know that you did the best you could with the resources inside yourself and outside at the time.

When you forgive yourself for the mistakes you made in the past, you free yourself up to learn and move on. You will not waste energy on regret that will not change anything and that makes you feel bad in the process. Remember that regret is needing the past to be different than it was!

Learn to be your own compassionate best friend. If you cannot be compassionate with yourself, you will find it hard to forgive others.

TRY THIS:

1. Remember a mistake that you made that you might still be beating yourself up for.
2. *Pause* and breathe, until you are able to calmly observe your thoughts about the mistake.
3. Imagine that someone you know and love had made the same mistake.
4. Imagine telling that person how you feel about the screw-up.
5. Now observe yourself making the same error. Observe how much harder you are on yourself.
6. Observe yourself from the perspective of a kind, compassionate, ideal parent or friend. You have just such a loving understanding attitude in your centre. Allow yourself to feel it surround the part of you that made a mistake.
7. Forgive yourself. If you learn from your mistakes, they are never wasted.

CHANGE YOUR EXPECTATION OF WHAT LIFE IS LIKE

Rather than busy mind all day with only reprieves when you remember to *Pause*, expect your "normal" to be a state of calm that only gets interrupted by thoughts and events.

When you feel grouchy, anxious, or any negative emotion, take a breath and observe your thoughts in that moment. Chances are good that your thoughts are responsible for your feelings. They may be reacting to whatever is happening in the moment, or they may just be resurrecting old fears and unresolved issues, bringing them back so that you can chew on them again.

Books, the internet, and friends all have ideas about what works. There are no rules—find what works for you. *Pause*, meditate, and practice bringing the quiet place into your life with patience, compassion, and loving kindness.

PRACTICE...

Whenever you feel a negative emotion, *Pause,* and observe the thoughts that are feeding it.

If you began by extending *Pause* into a five-minute quiet time morning and evening, consider adding a couple more of those to your day; or extending some of them to ten minutes; or if you begin to really enjoy this quiet place, you may want to treat yourself to longer periods of meditation.

EXPAND YOUR TOOLBOX ...

Experiment with what helps you into the quiet place:

- Focus on every breath
- Do a body check; begin with your head. Feel a wave of relaxation spread through your scalp, over your face, down your neck, though your chest, belly, back, hips, legs, and feet. If any part of your body is painful or tense, breathe into it giving it extra loving attention. You can also do this by beginning with your feet and bringing the relaxation up through your body.
- Use a mantra or count your breaths to distract your mind and feelings.
- Use imagery of a positive quiet place, often in nature.

NATURE HELPS

Rooted in the earth
Soaring to the sky
Moving my heart in sun filled inspiration
Bathing my soul in silence

The tree is real
My thoughts are not

I wrote this chapter while I was caring for my husband at home, when we lived in a forest with a river going by the end of the property. Nature helped me though that time and remains a beloved support system as I experienced the death of my husband and daughter:

I am blessed to have a forest, my favourite teacher, outside my window. I *Pause*, allow my breaths to move through my body, taking tension with them as they leave. I stare out at my favourite Douglas Fir, rooted in the earth; she soars silently into the sky, through wind, rain, and snow. I feel her strength and calm acceptance become a part of me. Without explanation, this model of *being* seeps into my awareness as separation between me and the tree begins to disappear. I feel her life force, her calm acceptance of this moment just the way it is. I sit and breathe with her. She has no thoughts, and since she is my teacher in this moment, I don't either. I allow my gaze to embrace the family of nature living around her and feel included in the harmony of life, without interference from my usual internal commentary.

Nature teaches me stillness. She shows me the way to my centre, my core, and my soul. She reminds me to go beyond my thoughts to find answers to questions and relief from stress. She gives me a sense of belonging that calms my conditioned fear of being alone, wrong, lost, overwhelmed, and all the other emotions that can so easily assail me as I travel this difficult path of being a 24/7 caregiver.

Plants and animals don't have a separate sense of self; they just belong. They help me to see past the persona manufactured by my mind that requires so much maintenance!

In spite of all the control I think I have, I didn't create my body. The same force that created the tree created me. It causes the tree's sap to run and my heart to circulate blood to every part of my body. When I feel this connection to nature, I am inspired by the unquestioning joy of a flower that blooms with no thought of how long it will last. I feel gratitude for the generosity with which nature feeds me and for her quiet dignity and acceptance of each moment just the way it is.

In a city, where much of nature is paved over, I find joy in the tenacity of blades of grass emerging through cracks in a sidewalk. If I am in a room without a view, I invite a houseplant or even photos of nature to be with me and help me stay on track.

The same silent space that holds nature, holds me. Only my thoughts separate us.

TRY THIS:

1. Go to a park or forest or lake or ocean if you can. If you can't get outside, sit with a houseplant or a photo. If you don't have an indoor plant, please consider getting at least one. If you have a pet, they would love to help you with this.

2. *Pause,* allow your breathing to move through your body relieving tension with each exhale. Really observe your body. You are aware of your breath now, but most of the time you breathe without awareness of your body's amazing machinery. Like everything in nature, we function without human attention.

3. Sit with the realization that the same life-force energy runs through you and nature. Most of your DNA has the same structure. Animals have bodies that function much like yours and brains that register pain, fear, and joy in the moment. They can model stillness because unlike you, they don't have the same cerebral cortex to create worry about whether they made a mistake or will be good enough.

4. Experience the amazing connection you have with nature.

5. Imagine what it would be like to be a tree or a plant that does not have a mind to produce worry.

6. Focus on a tree or a plant until you are part of its stillness.

7. Breathe with nature; feel all the ways that we are alike. Keep watching the forest or tree or plant or even a photo of nature and allow your vision to blur. Sit very still, and if your attention wanders, allow your breathing to bring you back. In the stillness you may actually feel your boundaries begin to fade until you share the stillness that nature lives in. She welcomes you there.

PART II – HUMAN REACTIONS AND EMOTIONS

— *Time to Pause* —

When life gives us lemons
Are we making lemonade
Or pouting because we wanted peaches?

When we label life in the moment as "unfair"
We experience it as not ok
So we can't be happy

Our inner arbiter of what is "fair"
Chooses its own standards
Often supported by those around us

No matter what life gives me
If I don't need it to be different
I will be free of the suffering
My ego would add
To events that are already hard

So a Pause when it's tough
Breathe and show up with what IS
In freedom from thoughts
Of what's "fair"

INNER AUTHORITY

Observation of the thoughts that would control my life
Reveals directives, collected through a lifetime
Of navigating through the rules and preferences
Of the world I live in.
I am discovering an intuitive sage,
Patiently present, when thoughts are quiet,
Ready to guide me with loving wisdom.
She cares for all beings, including me.

Perhaps she is in Rumi's field:
"out beyond wrong doing and right doing…"

My "aha" moment one morning came about from an experience of the previous two weeks. I made a New Year resolution to get up at 6 a.m., start writing at 8 a.m., and write until noon, Monday through Friday. My friend Mary agreed to do the same, and we had been checking in with each other, encouraging each other, and sharing our experiences.

The first thing I noticed is that I hated getting up at 6 a.m., but around 7 a.m., I am ready. Doing yoga right before I start writing wakes up my intuitive writer. It's the one, I am discovering, who writes anything worth reading. At first, I cut short my yoga if it was going past 8, turned on my computer, and sat in front of it…and sat… my conditioned thoughts righteously satisfied that I was following the rules I had made. Yes, I made the rules… but…what part of me made the rules? I realized I had an internal conflict going on between my self-imposed authority and what really works for me. I wasn't alone with this experience, Mary's body weighed in to tell her internal boss it was out of line, by making her heart race when she was obediently trying to make her bed before her 8 a.m. self-imposed deadline!

Like all conflicts, there are ways in which both sides are right and have something valuable to offer. I hadn't been writing, so the deal I made with Mary encouraged me to get started again. "Thank you" to my thinking self for coming up with the system and getting it going. However, that part of me tends to be pretty rigid, and the system was not going to work unless I also listened to my quiet, intuitive centre.

Here is where *Pause* comes into the story. When I *Pause* and observe my thoughts, they are less pushy, and as they slow down, a feeling of calm begins to creep in. In that quiet place, I can just observe that my great plan is not working, and intuitive wisdom begins to bubble up. Would getting up around 7 a.m. work? Since I am not working for an external boss, I run it by my internal boss and realize I can get up at 7 a.m., start writing at 9 a.m., and work past noon if I am on a roll, or not. If I push past what is working, I will lose momentum. I reframe my yoga as part of my writing experience and will not cut it short.

I am pleased that after years of working with the exercise to *Pause*, and having written about the need for harmony between thoughts and intuition, I am still able to be pleasantly surprised by how well it works. I know I am not alone in wrestling with this particular conflict. I'm not the only one with an in-house critic and boss who doesn't look out for me or listen to the wisdom of my intuitive Self. Until I learned to observe my thoughts, the conflict was unconscious and sapped a great deal of the energy that could have gone into finding a solution that would honour me as well as the project and anyone I might have been doing the work for.

There are all kinds of messages floating around about logic being good and feelings or intuition being flakey. Now we also hear ego is bad and soul is good. I don't think we would have both unless they were both useful. My experience tells me that the best solutions and most successful projects are blessed by the integration of both. *Pause* creates a way to allow both to work in harmony.

TRY THIS:

1. Think of any project that you are currently involved with or that you might have had or will have recurring problems with.
2. Breathe; allow the breath to go through your body taking tension with it as it goes.
3. Observe your body.
4. Observe whatever thoughts are coming to you. Don't try to change them; just watch them as if they belong to someone else.
5. Into this quiet place bring in the image of your inner boss/critic.
6. Observe what it is telling you to do about the project, and the directions coming from this boss. Don't argue, just notice how you feel. Witness with compassion and gratitude your strategies for coping. Say "thank you."
7. Return to awareness of your breathing, and in the quiet left behind, when your thoughts cede the floor, allow your intuition to weigh in on the project your mind has been dealing with.

ANGER

A tiger
Prowling through my brain
Fed by fear
Which comes in many flavours.

Is anger optional?

If it's optional, I have a choice. I didn't have to respond in anger to a letter that I received before checking out all the facts. I read the letter and decided that the committee I was on had sent out a fundraising letter that ignored the values we had agreed upon. I didn't *Pause* before I sent an email making my thoughts on the matter known. I have spent a lot of time and energy since with damage control. All avoidable if I had taken time to *Pause* before reacting to my desire to have it done a different way/my way.

The letter is an example of a situation when there was lots of time to choose to *Pause* before acting. There are also situations when we are confronted with anger in the moment. I remember an incident one summer when I took my husband to the local farmer's market. The handicap parking spaces were all full. I pulled off to the side so that other cars could get around and proceeded to get the wheelchair out of the car. An irate man started yelling at me that I was not in a legal parking place, while I was struggling to get my husband into the wheelchair. I was shocked by his venom and could feel my fight-or-flight hormones suddenly raging. Yet there was still a choice. I could yell back at him, and no one would have faulted me for calling him any of the names that were going through my head...or I could make myself *Pause* and calmly tell him that I would move the car when I had my husband safely in the chair. Right now, as I write about the incident, I can feel the adrenalin. I can also feel the strength and well-being associated with not joining the man's anger.

Untamed, anger can cause a lot of trouble for me and pain for others. Even when it's justified, I would still like to *Pause* long enough to bring my wise Self in to help me express what I'm feeling or what I think needs to happen. I would like anger to become another blue dot—a signal to *Pause*.

That summer, when I had been caring for my husband at home for over three years, fatigue played a part in the way my mind responded to the above situation as well as to situations that I might have found innocuous at other times. I was tired from being up in the night and realized that my fuse was short. Knowing this, I insisted that I *Pause* before I reacted so that I wouldn't get embroiled in battles that didn't need to be fought and would take even more energy from my precious supply.

We live in a world where a fast pace is valued and expected. It almost feels like we have been given the right to be angry when things don't go our way. Have we turned into a narcissistic nation where the world revolves around us to such an extent that we believe we control time and events and they should always be to our liking? If we believe that, then anger follows, often the most annoying kind, righteous indignation! I once read that one minute of anger equals sixty seconds of unhappiness.

I think there is a general misconception that anger makes us stronger, more powerful, and that if we don't respond in anger, we will be weak and taken advantage of. I am here to tell you that I have never felt more powerful than when I refused to join the man's rage in the parking lot.

Sometimes our anger seems to protect us from fear. Getting in touch with our fear when we are angry might feel dangerous. I have found, however, that I feel much more empowered when I *Pause* and pay attention to my breathing during a fight. Incidentally, it often seems to have a calming effect on the person who is angry with me too.

TRY THIS:

If you find that you are angry with someone or a situation, *Pause,* observe your thoughts, and answer these questions:

1. What are you telling yourself about your adversary?
2. What are you telling yourself about you in the midst of the anger? Are you telling yourself that you must not be important or that there is something wrong with you if your adversary is treating you this way?
3. What change are you asking for?
4. What change might you be willing to make?
5. Ask yourself what you are afraid of. Observe the fear and breathe into it from your powerful centre.
6. When you encounter anger in someone else, see if you can determine how that person may be threatened, and *Pause.*

— *Time to Pause* —

I want you to love me
But I am afraid that you don't
In fear
I crawl into my cloak of anger

I was hurt as a child
You were hurt as a child
Two hurt children
Looking for love

I am getting to know a place of stillness
It is filled with enough love and compassion
To heal both of us
I will meet you there

Please come as you are
I understand that it will take
A long time to trust that I wait for you in stillness

REINTERPRET THOUGHTS THROUGH A MINDFUL LENS

Flashback Experience

Right now, I am in Santa Fe, NM, the city where Will and I spent our honeymoon and where we came often for romantic get-away weekends. I am here alone and have been told that Will is palliative. I am assailed by memories, the smell of pinion fires, roasting green chilies, the intense blue skies, dramatic sunsets, favourite restaurants; every street carries an imprint in my mind of walking hand in hand. When I Pause here and observe my thoughts, I catch them whining about how we will never experience this magical place together again. When those thoughts subside, I feel a wave of almost overwhelming gratitude for all we experienced here. There are cleansing tears of grief and a smile of appreciation, and I recall Khalil Gibran's words, "When you are sorrowful, look again in your heart and you shall see in truth, you are weeping for that which has been your delight." Tears of gratitude and a Pause to cleanse the old sticky feelings of loss, and I am free to love this city with its treasure trove of memories.

Moments like this flashback can seem so real. My thoughts came in and caused pain in a situation that had the potential for gratitude and appreciation for precious memories and for healing grief—the grief that comes with cleansing tears, not weighted down by thoughts of regret and fear of the future. It seems like an example of the Buddhist saying that "pain is inevitable, but suffering is optional."

I believe it is possible, as we practice observing our thoughts through our mindful lens, which is the quiet place inside, to know when our thoughts are causing our suffering. It frequently gets easier with practice and can sometimes produce some lovely quiet moments. It will often result in a shift in mood because you have separated the mood from the thoughts that were supporting it.

TRY THIS:

1. *Pause* and identify the mood you are in at this moment, or recall the mood you woke up with this morning or one that brought you down recently.
2. Stand back and observe the thoughts that are supporting this mood.
3. Breathe and look around; observe what is real in this moment. Physically notice where you are. Be aware of your body. Is anything really happening to cause you distress?
   a. If there is something that needs to be dealt with, allow your quiet, wise Self to suggest what to do.
   b. If, as is most often the case, the moment is quiet when your thoughts are quiet, give yourself permission to just breathe and Be.
4. If your thoughts push back in, or the mood starts creeping back, repeat the process. *Pause*, breathe, observe.

CONFLICT INSIDE MY HEAD

When I listen to my thoughts, I sometimes hear a battle raging inside with no contributions from external sources. It's just between parts of me that disagree about what to do or how to be, or are beating me up for something I think I did wrong. My inner critic is pretty tough on me and hard to please. For example, when I return from a social gathering and *Pause*, I hear my head commenting on what I said or did, and it is seldom complimentary.

My thoughts also engage in altercations with others who have no input into the dialogue and would most often be surprised that I am fighting with them. Prior to an interview, if I *Pause*, I might hear my thoughts defending me, criticizing the interviewer, or fighting for my point of view. I get to the interview and realize the problems were invented inside my own head and have nothing to do with the person who is interviewing me.

After I *Pause* and observe my inner battles, I am most often able to see them for what they are and experience a sense of peaceful relief from the internal tension.

TRY THIS:

1. Carry a little notebook or, if you carry a mobile device, use the notebook in the device.
2. As you *Pause* and observe your thoughts throughout the day, jot down what you hear from inside. Notice how often you are privy to a fight of some sort being waged within.
3. Track the subjects of your internal conflicts for five days.
4. Note what patterns emerge.

EMOTIONAL PREFERENCES

Tough stuff happens
I get sad
You get mad
She gets guilty
He's going to fix it

Same trigger
Different reactions

Do you know what your emotional preference is when something goes amok? Do you know the preferences of the people you are closest to?

I recall an example that I can use to illustrate this. It occurred while I was caring for my husband at home during his long illness. The agency that manages the nursing aides who came in twice a day to help with my husband called a meeting here at our house to train the aides to use a lift with him. They didn't ask if the time was convenient or even tell me they were coming. I found out accidentally from one of the workers. I realize as I write about this that I felt a variety of emotions, and all of them stemmed from how my conditioned mind processed what was happening.

How dare they treat me with so little consideration?—all the energy of righteous indignation puffs me up like a rooster, sort of even feels good! Or I could feel sad that they have so little consideration for poor me, and that also feels a bit good. Or I must have done something wrong to deserve this kind of treatment, and that feels yucky. Or, I am furious; sort of the same as the first one; I feel the righteous indignation come in. Or I could get even and spread the word about the person who was supposed to call me about it and didn't. Or I can *Pause*...

When I *Pause*, I breathe and observe all those reactions. I can even trace them back to where I first learned them. Some feel pretty natural and some just aren't part of my conditioned repertoire. I recognize all of them for what they are. They are all coping mechanisms for dealing with difficult situations and, if unquestioned, will pop out automatically when an occasion triggers them. When that happens, I run the risk of hurting someone else and making the situation worse for myself.

I have been remembering to *Pause* for quite a while, so it now comes in automatically before I open my mouth in reaction. *Pause* allows me to choose my reaction from my centre rather than leaving my conditioned mind in charge to make a mess.

So staying with the example, when I was able to observe my conditioned response, I began to feel a sense of calm, a sign that my centre was now responding. From my centre came compassion for the overworked woman who forgot to call me; gratitude for the fact that the agency is going to provide a lift so that my husband will not have to stay in bed 24/7; gratitude that I can keep Will at home till the end, because of all these amazing people. It didn't take my centre long to actually make the mind-made upset disappear. What a gift my centre is. When they arrived later, we had a warm and productive meeting, and anger, guilt, sadness, and all the other negative emotions never raised their heads.

This is how I want to live! I want to live with love, compassion, and gratitude for myself and everyone I come into contact with. When I *Pause* and put my centre in the driver's seat, that is a realistic possibility, and when I slip, I want to feel that same compassion for myself.

TRY THIS:

1. Remember a time when you got angry, were filled with righteous indignation, or reacted to a situation in a way that felt bad to you and possibly made the situation worse.
2. Pause and create a new video allowing your wise quiet Self to be the director this time.
3. Whenever you are confronted by a difficult situation, instead of reacting from old negative conditioning, *Pause.* Take the time to decide how you want to react. What outcome would you like to see? How can you contribute to that outcome?

NOW

*There is no symbol for Now
On the face of a clock*

Now is what is happening while we are thinking about something else.

Now is happening while we are doing the things that we think we should be doing and putting off what we would really like to do.

So often at the end of the day, I wonder where it went. It was a beautiful sunny day, and I didn't go out for a walk. Was I really too busy to do that? Probably not. My situation may be different from yours because I am retired now and do have more choices about how to spend my time. But even when I was a single working mom and in school, and recently when I was caring for my husband at home, I can look back and see that I could have spent more time "smelling the roses," if I hadn't allowed my mind to obscure the present moment.

Showing up and really embracing life takes shifting awareness from the constant thoughts in my head and going into my quiet space where I am aware of "now." My quiet, wise Self may say that it is time to do the laundry, study, or do my taxes, and from that place, I will do those things while fully present with the task. Being in the moment while doing a task is so much more enjoyable than if I did it while wishing I was doing something else or worrying about something else.

Every time I *Pause* and observe my thoughts, I bring myself out of the squirrel cage in my head and into *Now*. My energy then flows from my wise Self. I am not in conflict with my conditioned mind. I appreciate and honour my mind for all is does for me. I am, in this moment, in harmony. I am aware of my thoughts and of the quiet space beyond my thoughts.

TRY THIS:

1. Allow yourself to observe whatever you are telling yourself in this moment about what you "should" be doing now and with the rest of your day or evening.
2. Give yourself some time to sit, breathe, and observe, as if you were a loving friend of your mind. Have compassion for how hard your mind works to make you fulfill all of your old conditioned "shoulds."
3. With some objective distance from the taskmaster in your head, you may be able to sort out what is important and what is not.
4. Is it possible to see what your relationship is with time?
5. Is there a place for *Now* in your life?

STRESS

My mind, the busy baker, takes the events of my life, stirs them around with my beliefs, previous experiences, and habitual coping mechanisms, and produces a large, messy bowl of stress. It takes so much energy to go about my day fighting my way through the daily concoction!

What if I could fire the baker or at least send her on vacation? After all, she works hard and has good intentions. She just needs a break and needs to get some perspective because what she is doing isn't working.

I am going to use *Pause* in order to breathe and observe the mess she is making. For example, I used this perspective when I was taking care of my husband during his last illness. His condition changed daily, so I was constantly trying to make solid plans around a moving target.

One morning, I was doing my yoga, and as the first light began to illuminate the woods outside my window, I drew a breath and realized I was hardly breathing. My head was stirring up stress using my husband's unpredictable condition and my habitual need to plan and control. Some desire to have more control of my life in this situation is reasonable, but it isn't going to happen the way my conditioned mind wants it. My energy can be more effectively used figuring out how to cope with things the way they are. As soon as I felt that acceptance, I felt my stress level go down. My mind moved out of battle mode and began to produce some ideas about how to help the situation.

We are really talking about the Serenity Prayer: changing what can be changed, accepting what can't be changed, and knowing the difference. When we *Pause* and observe our thoughts objectively, they calm, and the battle between what our mind wants and what is real also calms.

Most of us have a fear of letting go of the myth that we are in control and can force life to be the way our ego wants it to be. There is an amazing feeling of freedom and relief when we manage to actually see our need for control with perspective, take a breath, and open to dealing with the reality of the moment. In the quiet space that emerges as our thoughts begin to still, we have patience, tolerance, and compassion for what is happening right now. We then have options not available when our thoughts were demanding that we get our own way. I sometimes see my ego's demands—for example, wanting the rain to stop—like a demanding two-year-old. When I observe that two-year-old with compassion, possibilities emerge for enjoying a picnic in the rain!

TRY THIS:

1. *Pause* and observe your thoughts. Notice if your mind is doing battle with a situation that you are powerless to change in the moment. Observe how your mind deals with feeling powerless.
2. Now think of something that you really have no power over—like rain on your long-planned picnic.
3. *Pause* and observe your mind's response to the situation. You may notice that the thoughts are the cause of your stress.
4. As your thoughts become quieter, you may begin to feel yourself letting go of what your ego insists that you need—like a sunny day.

ADDICTIVE BEHAVIORS

Some hidden pleasures
Come with a price tag

In thought, I am lost
In stillness, I choose

I will not attempt here to address serious addictions and life-threatening dependence on alcohol, drugs, cigarettes, or even serious addictions to food. Learning to *Pause* may help in the treatment of serious addictions but would not take the place of professional help and a good treatment program.

I am going to apply the instructions to *Pause* to the more common addictions that many of us face sometimes. My own personal favourite is staying up too late, watching old movies, or reading and snacking. It seems like such fun at the time, though even while I am doing it, there is some awareness that I won't be happy with myself in the morning when I have to drag myself out of bed.

When we are tempted to eat or drink too much, or treat ourselves to some shopping we can't really afford, there is usually an internal dialogue going on about the pros and cons of these behaviors. This is why *Pause* can help. When we observe our thoughts objectively, we can see this internal argument more clearly.

Pause is like an invitation to be with a wise, intuitive, compassionate friend. This friend doesn't judge us but knows us, loves us just the way we are, and wants only the best for us. This friend is always waiting for us to notice him or her when we aren't listening to and believing our thoughts.

The loving compassion that exists in the stillness under our thoughts can help to heal our conditioned selves or egos. Our egos may carry memories of old, painful experiences of being unappreciated, unfairly treated, and controlled. They use these memories to justify why we deserve to indulge in unhealthy treats and behaviors. Our conditioned thoughts can be pretty persuasive late in the evening or if we are feeling unappreciated or misunderstood.

As we practice and integrate *Pause* into our lives, it will be there more often when we need it. As we go to the freezer for ice cream on our way to bed, we will eventually learn to *Pause* as we open the freezer door. Our witness will come into our consciousness more quickly and allow us to observe our behavior and even, perhaps, understand what part of our conditioned mind we are trying to feed. We might even notice that this poor, mistreated, misunderstood part has been leading us to the freezer for years and no amount of ice cream has comforted it.

The first time we turn away from the freezer empty-handed and head to bed early enough to wake up with energy the next morning, we may notice that decision feeds us in a way that the ice cream never has.

There can be a surprising sense of freedom and lightness of being when we choose to treat ourselves as a best friend rather than as someone who has no concern for our well-being.

It almost seems strange to use the word *freedom* because when we are reaching for the ice cream, there may be a part of us that feels like we have wrested our freedom from a boss or parent figure who might have tried to stop us from having what we thought we wanted. We may fool ourselves into thinking that we deserve the ice cream and the sense of "no one can stop me" may be hard to shake. With time, however, we may even become addicted to real freedom from the old voice in our heads that has been leading us to self-destructive behaviors in the mistaken belief that it would be freedom.

Make a deal with yourself to not indulge in a self-destructive behavior without first pausing, breathing, and observing what your mind is telling you. Notice I am not urging you to make a deal to just quit! I am suggesting that you initiate a mechanism that will help you to make healthy choices if you *Pause* and give it a chance.

TRY THIS:

1. The next time you are in a situation where you are tempted to do something that is not in your best interest, *Pause.* Take at least one or several deep breaths, allow your exhale to take tension from your body.
2. Stand back and observe. Listen to the dialogue in your head that is arguing for and against what you were about to do. Just observe and don't judge.
3. Show compassion for the part of you that wants to harm you—it is hurting. Compassion is not permission. In this situation, it is like a lovely wise friend who is always on your side.
4. As an outside observer with your best interests at heart, take note of any clues that you now have that can help prevent a recurrence in the future.
5. If this process allows you to resist the temptation, note how good that feels.
6. If you go ahead and indulge, just note how you came to that decision and realize that you are in charge. Don't beat yourself up.
7. If temptation lies inside the refrigerator or somewhere in the kitchen or a cabinet anywhere in the house, put a blue dot on the door to remind you to *Pause* before you open it.

PROCRASTINATION

Deep within me shines
Desire to embrace this precious life
With health, creativity, and purpose

In any conflict, it is important to identify the opponents and understand with compassion what they are fighting for. Find a compromise that serves the best interests of both. This applies to the opposing combatants inside my head.

My battle begins every morning before I get out of bed. "Lie here a little longer," says the Procrastinator. "Get up and enjoy the day and get lots done that you have been wanting to do," says my Lively One. Then when I do get up, it's to put on a robe and wander out to the kitchen to drink tea, snack on munchies, and aimlessly go from one diversion to another. (My Procrastinator at work.) Or get up, wash and dress, drink some tea, eat a light, healthy breakfast, exercise, meditate, and begin work on my book. (My Lively One.)

By noon, if I have followed my Procrastinator, I feel soggy and out of sorts, unless it is a day off after some productive ones. A morning flowing with the Lively One results in more energy to do things that allow outlets for my creativity and a feeling of contributing to life. I am more loving and compassionate with the world around me because I feel good about myself. Energy allowed to flow productively fuels the rest of the day.

I am finding that when I *Pause* and observe my thoughts as I begin my day, I stand back and see the conflict between my Procrastinator and my positive productive self. This has been changing my relationship with the old habitual thoughts about getting things done. I am gaining a fresh perspective. I don't fight them. I look at them with compassion and gratitude for how hard I have worked throughout my life to cope and succeed. I think of it as updating my "operating system" and unlike the new one on my computer, what I am learning from my intuitive Self is user friendly.

My wise Self is patient, not critical; it is my own internal, warm, loving friend. Solutions that come from this place feel like they are on my side. This intuitive Self, free of old conditioned messages from the past, can help me find my own reasons and rewards for doing what I do.

I am amazed that it is never too late to change a habit like procrastination.

TRY THIS:

1. Think of something that you frequently procrastinate about like exercise, balancing your checking account, writing a note to someone, doing the dishes, or whatever your favourite procrastination is.
2. As usual, start with a conscious breath and *Pause*. Observe the thoughts that come up when you know you are procrastinating.
3. Look at the thoughts with compassion; don't fight them, just observe them.
4. Allow the wise Self that lives in you to weigh in on what you would rather do than procrastinate.

NIGHTMARES

My brain at night
Sometimes makes up horror stories
Using just enough dregs of the day
To fill my off-duty sanity
With terror

Last night I woke at 1:00 a.m. in the clutches of evil beings out to destroy me. I was alone with no place to hide. Trapped with no one to help me. Slowly my awareness began to move out of the part of my brain that had taken over while I was sleeping. I woke up to the realization that I was in my cozy bed in the home where I feel safe, yet tentacles of fear kept trying to wrap themselves around my consciousness.

Because I have been working with *Pause* and using it throughout the days to move out of the clutches of old conditioned fears, I thought to use it to help me in the middle of the night. It was ready to help me move out of that aspect of my mind that can create havoc when I am not awake and watching it.

I took time to *Pause*, observed my body in my bed, observed my feelings of fear with compassion, observed the story of someone chasing me and trying to harm me. I slowed my breathing, my body began to relax, and I brought my awareness into the reality of the moment. Gratitude for the comfort and quiet I was surrounded with took over.

Thoughts, when observed from a distance, especially if we can do so with compassion, lose their veracity and the power to frighten us. I think of nightmares as an example of the ongoing thoughts that constantly run through my head. They are just more dramatic because our reality checker is sleeping on the job!

Some nightmares seem to have recurrent themes. One of mine is showing up for a test without having prepared for it. I have found that laying it out in the light of day with objectivity has taken some of the energy out of it, and I haven't had a repeat for some time now.

Some dreams seem to take our unsolved problems and weave them into stories that can help shine some light onto places where we are stuck. As an objective witnesses of these nighttime concoctions, we can sometimes gain insight into unresolved issues. Nightmares are just one more example of how our minds create our reality out of whatever old material they have in their closets.

TRY THIS:

1. Remember some old nightmares.
2. *Pause* and look at them objectively and with compassion.
3. Do you remember how it felt to be in their grip?
4. *Pause* now as you pull them back out of your memory bank.

TRY THIS WHEN YOU HAVE A NIGHTMARE:

1. *Pause*
2. See it with the distance of objectivity,
3. Retell the story. For example, if you dreamed that someone was chasing you, retell the dream in such a way that you are able to turn around and make them stop, or someone else comes to your rescue.

PART III – *PAUSE* WITH RELATIONSHIPS OF ALL KINDS

— *Time to Pause* —

A tiny drop of water
Illuminated by the sun
Contains every colour of the rainbow

Every cell in my body
Contains my DNA
The complete recipe for life

Every leaf, every pine needle
Every hair on the coat of the deer
Contains a complete recipe for life
Our recipes are almost the same

The same energy
Makes sap yellow
Makes blood red
In its absence
Sap and blood cease to flow

Together we live
Together we die
The same Grace fills us
In life and in death

RELATIONSHIPS IN STILLNESS

Words
From the trash heap in my head
I lock you in a cage of my assumptions
Let's meet in stillness

Will and I taught several meditation classes at our local elder college. From those classes we formed a meditation group that met biweekly for several years. We meditated together, and after meditating, we passed a "talking stick." We borrowed this tradition from Navajo people we knew in New Mexico. It fit our concept of listening from the quiet place inside rather than thinking about what to say when it is your turn, and speaking from the wisdom of your quiet place rather than from conditioned mind.

We shared about our meditation, what we learned, what worked and didn't work for us as we meditate. We shared our "aha!" moments, but we did not tell each other stories about our lives, though sometimes people shared a situation where being able to observe their thoughts helped them to deal with it.

The result was so rewarding. We learned to "love" each other in a way we all admitted was different than we had experienced before. It truly felt unconditional.

To know another human being, we don't need to know about them. We don't need to know their past, their beliefs, their financial or social standings. When we just know about someone, our minds come in and judge and assess them. Then we apply what we think we know about them to our own set of conditioned beliefs. We fit them into our frame of reference and relate to them through our own needs and fears.

Our mind-made assumptions relate to their mind-made assumptions. I lock you in a prison of my thoughts about who you are from the prison of who I think I am. I realize I have known some people for years and I do not feel as close to them as I did to the people in our meditation group.

Without the distraction of thoughts about someone, love can come more naturally in relationships. Love is then not chased away by all the reasons that our minds construct about why that person is not lovable, or why we should be afraid to let them in.

How does this apply to long-term relationships? We can't undo what we know about each other, but we can take the time to share silence with each other and discover each other in a new, clearer way when we are not listening to our thoughts.

Eckhart Tolle says, in his book *Stillness Speaks*, "Human interaction can be hell. Or it can be a great spiritual practice." The good news is that it is largely up to us whether it is hell or not. Even if you are mean or angry with me, I have control over how I respond and how I interpret the interaction, unless I leave my conditioned mind in charge.

One thing I can do to improve the way I relate to you is to *Pause* and observe my thoughts about me and about you, as I relate to you. Then I need to resist the temptation to tell you what I observed about you that causes me a problem! Instead, I take an objective look at my thoughts and determine how I might be contributing to the problem or seek a constructive solution.

During the time when I was a full-time caregiver, I became at odds with a very dear friend. I took the time to observe my thoughts and noticed that I felt she needed more from me than I had to give. My conditioned mind wanted me to be seen as a good person who is helpful and available. She picked up on that and was then upset with me because I couldn't deliver enough for her. I apologized for my lack of support for her, which helped me to set better boundaries and expectations based on the truth in the moment.

With some practice observing my part in various relationships, I realize that I am sometimes a chameleon, presenting what I think people want rather than showing up and sharing what is really important to me.

TRY THIS:

1. Invite a friend to meditate with you, or to just sit in silence in a quiet place. While you are there, *Pause*, breathe, and observe your thoughts until you find your quiet place. Share your experience.
2. Go into the woods and sit together in nature.
3. Before you meet with a family member, friend, or acquaintance, *Pause* and observe what your mind is telling you about the upcoming meeting.
4. After you have had an interaction, *Pause*, breathe, and observe what your thoughts are telling you about what happened.
5. If you take some notes about what you observe about yourself and others in relationships, you may see some patterns emerge and more quickly understand the dynamics and what you might do to change them.

ROMANCE

When I fall in love
I want to be sure
It's you I love
Not a fantasy I created to
Fill an empty place inside of me

As babies, having someone to love us is a survival issue. We don't arrive on the scene able to feed and take care of ourselves. Our need for love is deeply imbedded. Our minds talk to us about it a lot. They convince us to do all kinds of crazy stuff just so we can feel loved, long after we are independent. We are confronted by romance in the music we hear, ads for soap, cars, travel, etc.

When we have romance in our lives, it feels wonderful, so it is very natural to seek it out when it is not there.

This desire for romance can sometimes make it hard to hear our quiet wisdom. Most of us know about that wisdom later when we say "I knew better" after jumping headlong into a romance that turned out badly. The part of me that "knew better" is always available when I stand back and stop listening to and believing all my thoughts.

I know how hard it is to get past conditioned thoughts when falling in love. We artfully create a magical world designed to fill our deeply held wishes and desires. Objective information about what we are really doing and who the object of our passion is sometimes feels like a cold shower.

Being in love is not the survival issue our minds would have us believe. All the important ingredients for living a good life are inside of us. So being in a relationship is a choice. Years of my own personal experience and my work as a therapist have given me ample proof that living alone is far better than living with or being with the wrong person, and being with the right person is wonderful.

If I *Pause* and objectively observe what I am doing, I can prevent a headlong rush into a relationship with someone who actually exhibits traits that in wiser times I would never tolerate. Our wise intuitive Self can also spot the right person, sometimes looking beyond outward appearances and seeing the true beauty within.

There is often help available with this from a good friend or, heaven forbid, your mother, who says the object of your affection "sure drinks a lot," "likes to talk and doesn't seem interested in listening to you or your concerns," is "inconsiderate," and so on. They may not be right, but before fighting them off, *Pause*. When I hear the same kind of comments coming from my own still centre, I also need to *Pause*. From my objective observer, I try to understand both sides of the argument going on in my head.

When concerns are encountered during what I call the "limerence" phase, when everything is new and exciting, I so often hear the hope that the person will change. In my experience, most of us are on our best behaviour when the relationship is new and exciting, and anything that isn't working now will usually become more of a problem later, unless you are lucky enough to find someone who is open to problem-solve and change.

It feels so good to fall in love, and it is such an incredible gift to be in love with someone who enriches our life. Take time to *Pause* when falling in love and listen to that wise intuitive quiet place in order to have relationships that really work.

TRY THIS:

1. *Pause*, breathe, allowing each exhale to move through your body taking tension with it. Allow yourself some time to keep focusing on your breath and when you are relaxed and centred as possible, try one of the fantasies that follow:

2. If you are in the market for romance, take the time to have a fantasy about what you want. Imagine the qualities you would like in a partner, what kinds of things you would do together. Let your imagination run wild and enjoy your very own perfect romance. It will be more fun than reading a romantic novel, because you can make it come out exactly the way you want it.

3. If you have met someone and are beginning a relationship, have a fantasy about the relationship and in your fantasy, see it develop just the way you want it to. If you bump into your own value system or limitations based on who the person really is, take note about what you said you wanted and about how important his or her limitations are to you.

4. At the end of your fantasy, replay it for the kind, wise, loving parent inside of you. If red flags come up, take note of them. It may be possible for you to see more clearly if you are wanting a relationship to cater to your conditioned self or if you are ready to love unconditionally.

COMMITTED RELATIONSHIPS

My ego
Competes with your ego

My soul
Loves your soul
Sees your ego with compassion

My soul
Lives in serenity
So does yours

When the initial romance leads to a committed relationship, that relationship is precious. Our relationships can be the source of our greatest pleasure or the cause of our most acute pain. Our conditioned minds often go into them for the wrong reasons and create misunderstandings and unhealthy needs in even the best of them.

We often expect too much from relationships, wanting someone else to fill the empty place inside of us. The healthiest relationships occur between two people who are able to love, support, and respect themselves as well as each other.

Our true Self loves unconditionally without fear of being either overwhelmed or abandoned. My dog taught me a lot about this truth. She doesn't seem to have a constant avalanche of thoughts, beliefs, fears, resentments, and blame to dampen her outpouring of love. I doubt that she ever worried about being vulnerable when she loves. Her unconditional love brings mine to the surface. There are times when I looked at her or cuddled with her and felt my heart overflowing with a love that knows no boundaries. I also experience this in nature when my thoughts don't separate me and I just show up.

If we stop believing everything we think about our relationships, if we stop and observe and question every time we have a problem, we have a chance of relating at a level we might never have thought possible. Rather than taking for granted that a problem is too painful to deal with or indulging in fault-finding, *Pause,* breathe, and observe your thoughts. In the quiet place beyond those thoughts, there is a safe, calm place from which we can explore the relationship and the dynamics that are taking place in the moment.

When our ego is not in charge, we are not having to protect ourselves from the dangers our ego sees in the context of old hurts and experiences. We are free from old assumptions and fears about what will happen in a relationship and able to find new clarity about ourselves and the other person. Every time we *Pause* in a relationship and move beyond our conditioned thoughts about it, it is like we have created the possibility for a new beginning filled with compassion and forgiveness.

It's not always easy to figure out the dynamics of a misunderstanding when it occurs, especially if it has devolved into a fight. But moving from the old conditioned beliefs and coping mechanisms into the quiet place beyond thoughts gives us a chance to move past the old stuck places and possibly experience new ways of relating. When a problem arises, look first inside to see how you might be contributing to it. When you feel triggered, angry, want to lash out and hurt, *Pause.* Be willing to stand back and seek constructive solutions. Two people working together create much better solutions, than one person having to figure it all out.

Make finding the stillness inside of you a priority. When two people meet in stillness, a beautiful creation is formed that blesses both of you and everyone who comes in contact with you.

TRY THIS:

1. Invite your partner to *Pause* with you.
2. Set aside time to share quiet time to talk about your relationship. Begin with what's working for you and what you appreciate.
3. If there are issues that are not working for you, consider positive solutions and be ready to negotiate. Solutions are more apt to be available when you *Pause* rather than just allowing your conditioned mind to be in charge.
4. Even if your lives are very busy, make it a priority to have fun together. Remember the things you did while you were dating and falling in love? Bring them out of mothballs and do them again.
5. If your partner won't *Pause* with you, you can *Pause* and show him or her how it works for you. If they are not willing to try it with you initially, they might try it over time when they see how well it works for you and appreciate your calm approach to problem solving.

SEXUALITY

My sexuality
A gift of nature
Like the taste buds in my mouth
Treasure it
Enjoy it
Guilt, embarrassment and shame
Have no place among reactions
To the treasure nature gave us.

If *Pause* can release me from worry, guilt, blame, and all of the other messages and emotions that mess up my life, what could that same freedom do for my sexuality?

Sexuality, like every topic in this book, is apt to be messed up by our conditioned mind. If we had never received any information about how we were supposed to feel about it, it might just add pleasure to our lives. We have, however, been getting messages about our bodies and our right to enjoy them ever since we reached down to touch ourselves as babies because it felt good and had our hands smacked.

Our culture and religions have weighed in on the topic and made it sometimes an issue of abuse, power, or shame. The culture has used it as the focus of ad campaigns to sell almost anything. Sexual abuse has ruined the experience for far too many.

My discovery of cultures that celebrated the feminine and sexuality as a life-giving force helped to free me from the conditioning my mind had been exposed to. These cultures believed that sex was not shameful nor to be hidden, and women were not inferior nor meant to be punished for eating an apple, as I was taught as a child in Sunday School

I was fortunate to be able to travel to some of the places where archeological evidence of these societies still exists. In the prehistoric caves in France, the Greek Islands, and throughout Europe, I saw evidence of a time when sexuality was free of the beliefs that have interfered with the natural enjoyment of sensuality. The predominant beliefs that govern Western culture have only been around for 2000 years. That is just a "drop in the bucket" when you consider how many years humans have been living here.

Our culture and personal experiences of sexuality have formed belief systems and automatic reactions to our sexual experience. For some, taking time to *Pause* and getting to know what we are telling ourselves about sex might help. Our minds play an important role in our ability to enjoy the gift nature gave us.

TRY THIS:

1. Set aside a quiet time and observe what your mind says about sex.
2. For those who have experienced sexual abuse, I'm not suggesting that *Pause* alone will bring relief, but it may contribute to the healing process.
3. No matter what you discover as you listen to what your thoughts are telling you about sex and sensuality, try to imagine what your mind would be saying if you lived in a culture that celebrated sex as nature's gift.
4. *Pause* and breathe into your body seeing it as the temple you live in in this lifetime.

FRIENDSHIP

My friend
You are there with a shoulder
When I want to cry
Have faith in me
When I doubt myself
Have my back
When the going gets rough
Laugh with me
At our private jokes
I trust you so much
We can even fight and make up
You tell me when you think I am wrong
So I believe you when you think I'm right
You are a gift in my life.

Friendship is now recognized as contributing to a healthier and longer life. Our ability to form meaningful friendships is affected by what our thoughts tell us about our role and the roles of the people we would like to relate to, so a *Pause* can have a positive impact on our ability to relate to friends.

I doubt that the opportunity to collect "friends" and "likes" on social media quite meets our healthy, natural need for connection. If you find yourself checking your phone often for "likes," it might be helpful to *Pause* and observe your thoughts when you do it. If you notice a sense of anxious anticipation as you open your phone and a deflated or down feeling if your posts have failed to collect marks of attention, you may be spending time looking for approval from strangers and casual acquaintances that you could have spent reaching out to others on a more personal level.

For me, a real friend is someone who really listens and wants to know what is important to me. They will share openly about what is important to them as well, but there is a balance. I find when I get off the phone with a friend, I often have a smile on my lips. I look forward to talking to them and find myself thinking about them. A real friend is someone I like to be with when the going gets rough or there is something to celebrate. Most of us will only have one or at least a very few people with whom we feel this degree of connection and support.

I also have meaningful acquaintances. These are often people I share an interest with. We might hike together, work together, enjoy the same kind of music, or belong to the same club or community committee. We might just enjoy each other when we are involved in the same activity, or we might find other ways to connect. These acquaintances sometimes turn into deeper friendships. I often think the best way to meet new friends is through getting out into the community and becoming involved. We then meet others with similar interests.

We may have unreasonable expectations of friendships or be unwilling to negotiate boundaries that work for us. My ego may be seeking reinforcement or need to be right at another's expense, and the list goes on. My thoughts may be my best source of information about why friendships are difficult to form or sustain. When I think back to what has happened to rupture a friendship in the past, chances are there is a pattern, and I can learn a lot by being willing to look at it.

TRY THIS:

1. *Pause,* breathe, and observe your body. Allow each exhale to take tension with it as it leaves your body.
2. In this quieter place, ask yourself where you stand on the issue of friendships. Observe what your thoughts tell you.
3. If you realize you have good friends and are comfortable with these relationships, ask why you think this is true. You are doing something that is working for you; take note.
4. If you wish you had more or better friendships, ask your mind to show you a review of what you believe about friendships and about yourself as a friend. Do you blame others or yourself for your lack of comfort with friendships? If this is the case, you might want to write out those beliefs.
5. Friendships can evolve and change with time as people change jobs, marry, have children, etc. Sometimes a *Pause* can help you to adjust and find new ways of relating rather than assuming, for example, when your friend has a new baby that he or she is no longer a good friend.

FAMILY

I love my family
From a primitive depth

If I also like them,
Would seek them out as friends
What a bonus!

We grow together then scatter
Change values and life style
When we regroup
May we see each other anew

My conditioned mind is attached to my family like glue. Its deepest and most intractable lessons were learned in their midst. As an adult, I flew from the nest and now when I go back, I am often filled with conflict and disappointment as I try to reconcile my early lessons with what I learned from my exposure to the wider world.

For example, family holiday gatherings anticipated with excitement and dread can bring together dear people we have loved since childhood and who now sometimes drive us crazy! Our minds bring into these occasions a load of expectations of how we are supposed to behave and how they are supposed to be. We share the impossible wish to recreate the dreams of childhood or in some cases a dread of having to endure painful memories and recreations of the past.

But there is hope. What if we didn't allow our conditioned minds to tell us how to behave in order to gain the approval we always hoped for and don't believe we will get? What if we let go of preconceived ideas of who our family members are and how the gathering will play out? What if instead, we *Pause* and observe what our minds are generating when we get together with family.

Breathe and observe the video of what we think is to come. With the distance of objective observation, our thoughts and feelings about it calm, and we invite our quiet wise Self to the video of this interaction. You might find yourself able to maintain your centre no matter what happens or you might even decide to leave rather than subject yourself to painful treatment. The key is that whatever you do in this video that you are in charge of, you do from centre.

I can just imagine walking through the door centered in wisdom, love, and compassion. I read that line again and breathe into it. I can begin to feel it. My smile would be natural because I feel loving, nonjudgmental of myself and those I meet.

Whenever we come from our centre, we are more loving and compassionate. Others pick up on that and may respond in a more positive way to us than they otherwise would, but we can't let that be the reason for doing it. When we are centered and in the present moment, we meet everyone without preconceived ideas about who they are and how they will behave, so we are not walking in with our guard up. If I am more accepting and kind to you, you will likely respond in kind.

I try to see everyone's loving compassionate centre whether they know they have one or not. I love the term *Namaste*, which essentially means, "I bow to the god in you from the god in me." In this context, I would say, "I bow to you from the centre of me to the centre in you."

TRY THIS:

1. Try a fantasy rehearsal before you meet with family or attend a family holiday gathering.
2. *Pause* and allow your image of the meeting to be as positive as you can imagine, even if that means calmly leaving if that is best.
3. Breathe and observe whatever thoughts come up for you about family gatherings. Stand back as if you were a guest invited to objectively observe the event.
4. Now see yourself centered, loving, and compassionate with your family. No matter what they do or say, you are balanced and centered and able act with calm consideration for what is best for them and for you.

PAUSE WITH YOUNG CHILDREN

Parents and children
Who Pause together
Find the soul connection
That endures
The inevitable separations
On the road to adulthood

Can you imagine how much easier, productive, and fun our lives would have been if our parents had taught us how to quiet our thoughts and trust our wise, loving and compassionate centre?

Let's imagine doing that for our kids! I believe there is a greater need now than ever before to help children to know their inner world. Just like adults, children need time out from all the devices that constantly demand their attention. Whenever there is a lull, it seems we and our children reach for a cell phone or other device to check social media, text someone, or play a game. Many kids also have lessons, sports, and other activities in addition to school that fill all their waking hours. Most of them don't have time to play in the ways that would develop their imagination. They lack the space to discover the inner world where they can be comfortable without being entertained. They also need the experience of physically playing with toys that help them to learn to problem solve without consulting Google.

I recently had the experience of being with a three-year-old child who was growing up without techy toys. She had some fabric scraps, pebbles, sticks, leaves, and a simple doll, and she played by herself for long periods of time, making up stories. When I asked if I could play too, she welcomed me into her world, and we made up stories together. I had such fun with her.

I often find with other children who are entertained and kept busy externally that I have difficulty making a connection with them. They look outside of themselves for fun and diversion and do not develop trust in their ability to be with themselves and truly connect with others. There are advantages to some of the computer toys, and in order to function in the world that awaits children, they need to develop the quick reflexes learned from playing with them. Perhaps we need a balance of time for inner and outer activities.

I have noticed that many parents have difficulty setting limits on the amount of time their children, especially teenagers, spend with their cell phones. The teenage years are the time to push the limits, and in order to do that, they need limits to push against. Love your children enough to withstand their displeasure when they can't have what they want when they want it!

Here are some ways to relate differently:

- Read to your child and encourage them to love and discover books, the old-fashioned kind they can hold in their hands and look at the pictures.
- Sit with them and see what they are finding on the internet. There may be some very valuable things that will help your child to learn and develop, but there may be violence, bullying, and negativity even in some of the apps made for children.
- With children of all ages, including the teenagers who often pull away from the family into their own world, sit down to dinner together without cell phones. Talk to each other about your lives. Praise and encourage.

If arguments arise, *Pause* together. Value non-judgment, active listening, compassion.

As we develop our own ability to *Pause*, quiet our thoughts and build trust in our own centre, it becomes easier to it with our children.

Bring out the blue dots that you learned about in the beginning of this book. Remember, they helped you to make *Pause* a habit. Kids like those dots and have been known to help remind their parents to use them when they experience how much nicer it is to deal with parents who are in their quiet centre. In the process, they find their own. Even a toddler can learn to *Pause*.

TRY THIS:

1. Sit with your young child in a playful mode, with giggles and hugs.
   • Put a blue dot on your forehead and one on your child's forehead.
   • Take an exaggerated breath and let your eyes close.
   • Ask your child to take a breath with you.
   • Take some breaths together allowing your eyes to close each time and leaving a longer *Pause* at the end of the breaths.
   • More giggles and hugs and praise for how well it was done
2. Sit in nature together
   • Make a game of listening to discover how many new sounds you can hear. Look together and see how many colours you can name.
   • How many insects can you identify?
   • Help a child learn to appreciate the world that has nothing to do with a computer screen.
3. When your teenager is wrestling with relationship or other problems, teach them to *Pause* and observe the drama as if they were watching a video.

ALONE OR LONELY

In silence
I am not alone
I am free
From the mind
That disconnects me

Flashback:
Listening to my conditioned thoughts, I can feel painfully
lonely. A series of strokes have taken my husband—best friend
and soul mate—to a simple place where almost everything we
shared—ideas, work, play, and loving—have slipped from his
radar screen. I can still hug his warm body, as long as I don't
block his view of the TV screen. I know he won't be in his
body much longer. When that happens, I will be alone. When
my thoughts move in and take over, I can almost feel a panic.
My mind believes that being alone is a scary place to be.

I wrote the first paragraph while my husband was ill and I was caring for him at home. I finished this chapter several years later. My husband died in 2019, my golden retriever died in 2020, and my daughter died in 2021. I have written a lot about grief and won't focus on that here. However, as it impacts loneliness, there is something common to both grief and loneliness. When I am listening to my thoughts, they intensify my grief and they are the author of loneliness.

As I *Pause*, I find the pathway to the quiet place inside me is getting smoother. When I am in that quiet place, I may be physically alone, but I am not lonely.

When I do feel lonely, if I *Pause* and observe my thoughts, they are telling me all the reasons why it's not okay to be alone. My thoughts come up with reasons that may be different than yours. They are based on my own history and life experiences and the beliefs that my mind has constructed from those, though there are also messages that our culture gives us about being alone. There are also times when I am more vulnerable, like early evening right after dinner. I do miss having someone to watch a movie with or rehash the day, but if I don't allow my thoughts to take over, I won't wallow in self-pity. I will find a good book, or enjoy that movie by myself, or even talk to a friend on the phone.

Now that I am learning to trust that when those feelings of loneliness arise, I can *Pause* and find my quiet place where I know I am not alone. I am home. With awareness we can find the right balance of being out in the world and in stillness. As you feel better about yourself, less afraid of living alone, you may also find a good balance of creating social contacts and being at peace when alone.

TRY THIS:

1. Check in with your belief systems about what being alone means to you, and write your thoughts down.
2. Allow yourself to feel what loneliness feels like to you.
3. *Pause*, and observe those feelings with compassion.
4. Now surround feelings of loneliness with love and compassion; you will begin to understand why you are never alone in your quiet space.

PAUSE

PART IV – *PAUSE* FOR CAREGIVERS; *PAUSE* FOR GRIEVING

PAUSING WHILE CAREGIVING

I wrote this during a week-long respite during the time I was caring for my husband at home. I used the respite the way I most needed to—I gave myself a silent retreat. During the retreat, I used what I was writing about and called it a *Pause* Retreat.

Often when I write in my journal, a sort of poetry seems to come out of the quiet place inside of me. This is what came to me during that retreat:

For three years, my life has been lived around yours
For forty years, you have graced my life, filled my heart.
For the first time in nine months,
I am alone, exhausted in mind, body, and spirit,
I eat, I sleep, I write,
Just now, I picked up a book of Mel's poems and cried blessed
    tears.

You, my love, embraced death for years;
Until you came near it.
From up close, it must look different.
Your mind damaged by strokes, can't tell me.

You have lost your ability to travel alone.
You need me to dress and care for your body
My time and energy is dedicated to your final journey.
We are in this together, the way we have always been.

I sit lightly on your lap, you wrap weak shaky arms around
    me.
My heart opens and breaks.

You still love me, the woman, your soul mate, your
  playmate...and
Some of that love is for a mother who cares for you now.

My grief so confused, I face the loss of my beloved best friend,
Then you show up again...sometimes a beloved stranger.
I want to be mindful, love who you are in this moment,
Be with my grief when you are gone in the next.
I am drained of emotion, needing silence to heal.
Working to care for your failing body and mind
Fills my time...I get lost...
Losing you, I lose me.
I try harder to take the tiller on these rough seas of our lives,
Yet you were the sailor.

WHAT HAPPENS WHEN YOU HIT THE WALL

Exhausted
Emotionally drained

Centre...
Where are you???

Being a caregiver doesn't stop when you get a bad cold and feel pulled like a magnet to sleep...*please...just let me sleep.* My centre is like a guttering candle. Flickers of calm confidence and trust are extinguished by the power of my mind to overcome my weakened state, grab my body's pain, and turn it into an overwhelming drama of helplessness. The Wall!

I realize that often when I *Pause* and observe my thoughts, I am actually trying to stop them or change them, even though I know I can't win a battle with my mind and need to just observe its output. I also know that when I try to change my thoughts, I am not really moving into my centre. My mind is messing with my mind.

When I am in trouble, I need the same thing from myself as I need from someone outside. Just listen. Stand back and observe with compassion the pain or exhaustion. Be there, don't go running off looking for Band-Aids. My centre hasn't gone anywhere, and if I just breathe into it, soon I will feel the soothing balm of stillness. Just stopping the dramatic thoughts frees up much needed energy.

If you ever feel this state of overwhelm, please know you are not alone. Please know there is a way to gain some relief. One moment at a time, we can handle almost anything. It's our catastrophic thoughts that most often push us to the wall.

TRY THIS:

1. When any event in life pushes you to a place where you feel you just can't stand it, pull back and *Pause.*
2. Observe your thoughts and your situation with compassion. Allow your breathing to bring you into the moment where you can handle everything.

— Time to Pause —

Contentment
While waiting for the light to change

Satisfaction
While doing, not just later when it's done

Acceptance
When events are not the ones you planned for

Enjoying life while it's happening
Every detour is an opportunity to see new scenery

Patience is a delightful reward for mindfulness.

PAUSE FOR PATIENCE

Taking care of Will when he was ill taught me a great deal about patience. My decision to care for Will at home came with a commitment to do all I could to be patient with the process. Like most commitments, it wouldn't work to say it once and put it aside. I needed to consciously renew the commitment several times a day for over three years. The commitment to be patient came with a commitment to make *Pause* a part of my life, because when I *Pause* and slow my thoughts, patience flows from the silence that exists when my mind is quiet.

When I helped Will eat a meal, I needed to show up and be with the process, setting aside thoughts of what I should or might even rather be doing. Out of the patient approach came the satisfaction of bringing him pleasure and awareness of the love that fuelled the whole deal of having him at home. The impatient approach, fueled by the need to be somewhere else or doing something else, would take longer, and the regret would be so painful. Unfortunately, I know that from experience!

Over time I realized that there were certain things that I did for Will that tried my patience more than others. I tried to make sure to *Pause* before I began.

When anyone is ill or incapacitated, they are almost always going to be slower, need more careful explanations, and sometimes need the same explanations or directions over and over again. This makes caregiving a graduate school class in learning patience. I found I didn't have to wait for someone else to grade me on how well I was doing. If I was passing the course, everything flowed more smoothly, I was more relaxed, and Will was definitely happier and more cooperative. Like any good class, the lessons carried over to other things. I think that I became more patient than I used to be in general.

A stop light is an opportunity to *Pause*. Being kept waiting for an appointment is a gift of time, adding some meditation to the initial moment to *Pause*. It is time to be in my favourite place—stillness. With time not assigned to something else, I can stop and observe my thoughts until they subside, and I feel the luxury of my quiet place inside.

I don't think I have ever met a happy, impatient person. So there are many rewards for me when I *Pause* and develop patience. I love being with patient people and I want to be one too. Patience carries us through the long haul with grace, and we can learn it. Patience helps us to feel stronger, more competent, and it helps us avoid the behaviours that create guilt. We just plain do a better job when we are patient, and our inner critic has much less to chew on!

TRY THIS:

1. Look in the mirror and notice your face. Now *Pause*, breathe, and allow your breath to move through your body taking tension with it.
2. Take as many of those focused breaths as you need in order to feel your body relax.
3. Observe your thoughts until they slow down, and you can begin to feel the silence inside.
4. Look again at your face. Is your mouth more relaxed, possibly even a bit of a smile? Are your eyes softer?
5. When you *Pause* and your countenance changes, notice how you feel. Now go out among others with this same relaxed expression and note how others respond to you.
6. If you are a caregiver, approach the one you are caring for with your softened face, and notice how they respond.

TWO WAYS TO GRIEVE: FOR CAREGIVERS

A broken heart
Embraces truth
Of pleasure and of pain

Love flows forth and touches
Everything the same.

If I must grieve, I want my conditioned mind to stay out of it! The last thing I need heaped on top of a painful loss is my mind telling me that I am to blame, that the pain will be so bad I won't be able to stand it, or that my life is ruined.

Grief is an inevitable part of life and can help us grow or shut us down, depending on how we do it.

So I must grieve sometimes, even though my mind may be afraid to go there. Otherwise, the feelings about the losses will jam up my flow of energy like a drainpipe full of leaves in need of cleaning.

While I was caring for my husband at home, I often felt like I was on a grief roller coaster. During his illness, I often wrote about the process of caregiving and grief. The following is an essay I wrote at that time.

*　*　*　*

My husband's brain, besieged by strokes, sometimes clears, and my old love is right here with me, sense of humour and all. My heart opens, and I embrace the time I have with him. A few hours later, a stranger speaks to me from his body, and I feel such a loss—my lover, my friend, is gone, and I don't know if or when he'll be back.

My conditioned mind would handle this with denial, bargaining, and even anger, which would morph into guilt, especially if I vented it to Will or others. It would also push me to avoid the whole situation. It would have me stay busy and ignore the shifts, but I don't want to deprive myself of even short visits with this wonderful man.

So, I *Pause* a lot these days. Only when I observe my thoughts and come into the moment can I fully feel the grief and the love. Many poets have wisely said there is no grief without love, and I have never understood it as well as I do now. In the loving moments, I experience joy, and when they are gone, sometimes the grief feels like the bottom dropping out of my heart. When I stay with it and continue to breathe into my centre, the love that is always in my centre somehow softens the pain. It is still pain but not the kind of pain that my mind generates out of losses.

This rollercoaster experience of love and loss almost seems like a slow-motion lesson in grief. I am aware that when Will dies, I will have to go through a grief that will be more intense as I deal with the finality of my loss. I have had major losses before and felt many emotions— from anger and fear to sorrow and relief. Through all of the emotions, I will need to remember to keep breathing, keep taking time to *Pause*, and know that in my centre is the love and compassion I need to move through the grief to healing. I know it is important not to go into a spiritual bypass, which would mean avoiding my real feelings. I know instead how necessary it is to move through them.

I also remember the importance of taking care of myself physically, availing myself of supportive friends and family, just like I would if I was recovering from a physical illness.

As much as possible, we need to make time to grieve. Honour the process. I have found I need a simple way to proceed—to *Pause* in order to prevent my conditioned mind from taking over works for me. I hope it will help you as well.

TRY THIS:

1. Allow yourself to be aware of a current or past grief over a loss, and imagine it is a video that you are watching.
2. Pause the video.
3. Breathe and allow each exhale to move through your body, taking tension with it as it goes.
4. Observe your body
5. Restart the video about your loss in slow motion and observe your thoughts and feelings.
6. Continue to breathe and observe the video of your grief.
7. Be aware that there is a quiet place inside, perhaps a still point. In that quiet, there is love and compassion, like a kind, loving, ideal parent or friend who can surround you as you watch your grief. Stay with that image for as long as you can.
8. You may want to try this more than once until you are able to experience being loved and comforted by this beautiful energy right inside your own centre. Once you have this experience, you may never feel alone with grief again.

PERCEPTION

The nursing aide
Sitting on the bathroom floor
Washing Will's feet

Love fills me
Washes over this woman
My mind had labeled loud and bossy

I learned so much during the years I cared for my husband at home and wrote the following essay during that time:

The government-run home-support agency that allows me to keep my husband at home rather than having to place him in a facility has been a source of frustration and an incredible blessing. It has taught me valuable lessons in perception.

It made it easy for my conditioned mind to find the negative. For over a year, the managers did not understand the benefits of continuity of care, and in that time, sent out over 100 different people to care for Will. Each time a new person came, I had to show them the ropes rather than getting a break while they were here, and Will had to tolerate stranger after stranger providing his very personal care. My mind had a field day full of righteous indignation. I went online and found research studies extolling the virtues of continuity of care. I fussed and fumed, mostly silently.

All the while, almost all of these strangers were kind, caring people who performed difficult tasks with such grace. I would sometimes meet them at the door and warn about a mess, and they never failed to say that it was ok and that was why they were here. I would then hear them talking to Will, treating him with dignity and respect, no matter what they were doing for him.

I didn't want all these strangers in my private space, *and* I am filled with gratitude and humility in the face of their grace.

Staying in touch with appreciation doesn't mean that I can't problem-solve the issues that are difficult. It just means that it isn't helpful to anyone if I allow my conditioned mind to focus on what doesn't work and allow it to drown out the loving compassion that my soul has to offer.

I am learning so much about how different the world seems from my judgmental, often negative, conditioned mind, and what is possible when my mind is quiet and my soul can weigh in. Wisdom and feelings generated from the soul feel so good!

Our troubled world needs us to bring that into our daily lives. Imagine politics, if politicians brought their love and compassion to the table, looking for the best in both sides of the arguments. What if we as voters refused to accept the rhetoric of our own party and insisted on a positive approach to getting things done? If we all go inside and listen to our thoughts about race, gender, nationality, religion, could we identify our prejudices and turn them around?

TRY THIS:

1. Think about something that is bothering you, from a neighbour with a barking dog, to something your loved one does that is annoying, or a rule that doesn't make sense or the way the medical community red tape impacts you...

2. *Pause* and observe your thoughts on the subject. Stand back as if you were listening to a stranger tell you about the annoyance. As you pull farther and farther back from the diatribe in your head, breathe and feel yourself getting calmer until you find yourself actually observing this issue through the loving eyes of your soul.

3. Notice your perception of the issue when you are not listening to your conditioned thoughts.

MINDFUL GRIEF

When Will, my husband, my lover and my best friend of over forty years, died on January 19, 2019, I had been discovering and practicing a way to shift my awareness from my thoughts to the quiet place inside of me while I cared for him at home.

More than ever before, I needed to know the place inside of me that knows this moment isn't really the frightening scenario my mind presents. *Pause* is a form of meditation on the run.

With practice, this process has become easier, and it increasingly results in more access to the quiet wisdom always present when my thoughts are not drowning it out. This helped me to stay centered when two years after Will died, my precious daughter, Erin, became gravely ill. It was during the covid pandemic, and I was not allowed to visit her in the hospital until they determined that she was dying. She was in pain and ready to let go by the time I was able to be with her. I will always be grateful that knowing how to stay in my compassionate centre allowed me to really be there for her. Even though my grief was beyond description, I did not share it with her in a way that would have increased her own suffering. We cried together as we expressed our love and appreciation for each other and did what still seems impossible—we said goodbye. I have more than made up for the expressions of grief since then, but I have *Pause* to help me when my thoughts would come in and torture me with possibilities about how I should have been able to save her

I went back through journals written through the years of loss. I saw that most of what I had written expressed how my grief was affected by my commitment to *Pause*—my ability to witness the thoughts of remorse, guilt, and fear of loneliness with compassion, and then experience the wisdom and serenity when I stopped listening to the noisy outpouring of my conditioned self.

I have been learning the difference between grief in my head and the primitive outpouring of grief, often accompanied by deep cleansing tears. That insight often greets me now when I pause the thoughts that would torment me about how I should have been able to prevent the deaths of my precious loved ones.

This practice has helped me so much to get through the last eight years of caring for my loved ones as they died, then experiencing life without them. It is not an escape from the grief that pours straight out of my heart —the kind that seems often to be triggered by a piece of music, a sight, or smell, or a comment, or very often a kindness—and results in a deep outpouring of tears. I welcome those tears and am learning not to apologize for them. I often feel cleaned out by them, sometimes exhausted. They are the real healing grief. The following exercise is not meant to bypass that part of grief. It is, however, a way through the incessant thoughts generated by our conditioned mind about fear, guilt, loneliness, and all the other feelings and beliefs that contaminate the pure grief of the loss of our loved ones.

TRY THIS:

1. Imagine a loss.
2. *Pause*, breathe, and observe your thoughts and feelings with compassion.
3. If possible, give yourself some time to feel compassion and love for yourself, just as you would for a precious

family member, friend, or even a stranger who was experiencing a loss like yours.

4. Try to access the gratitude you feel for the time you had your loved one in your life. If you are grieving for that person, they must have been a gift in your life while they were alive. Kahlil Gibran says that the more precious they were, the harder we grieve for them.

THE CURATIVE POWER OF COMPASSION

The healing balm of compassion
Flowing from my loving heart
Wraps my own pain in grace.

In a period of three years my husband, my daughter and my golden retriever all died. When my daughter died, at one point I was sobbing so hard, I thought I would throw up! Just at the moment when I feared I would never stop crying, I remembered being with a cow after the dairy farmer had taken away her calf. She was bawling! I remember the deep compassion I felt for her. I felt my heart breaking for her. With this memory, I was suddenly filled with the same compassion for myself. I was no different than the cow. Like her, I am a mother who lost her child.

Somehow the memory of the cow reminded me that all beings have a primitive, built-in love for their offspring. I wonder if it is built into our DNA for the survival of our species. As humans, does it help us through those moments when those precious babies are two years old, and we are tearing our hair? With this realization, I have a powerful understanding that I am not alone with this pain that sometimes feels unbearable.

It's difficult to describe how this flood of compassion, which came from deep in my own heart, filled me. I know it's not unusual for me to feel loving empathy for others, and I have been on the receiving end of heartfelt mercy from beautiful people in my life and even strangers. That too is precious and so very healing. But this compassion for myself was different. It was an inside job. It shut out any thoughts of guilt, regret, anger, and even softened the fear that maybe I couldn't stand this much pain. The tears that had been pouring from the depths of my being seemed, in that moment, to clean out the well of despair I had been drowning in. I felt filled with a kind of grace, which I am beginning to recognize also contains an acceptance of what is real in this moment. I can't bring my daughter and my husband back. This sense of loving compassion encompasses that truth and brings a feeling of peace that I had not known would be possible to feel again.

It's not a permanent fix. Now when I fall into the well of despair, which can be brought on by so many different triggers, I often bring back the memory of the cow. Sometimes, with practice, I am able to just feel the memory of the loving empathy in my heart, which includes me. When the grief comes up, I *Pause*, breathe, and observe the thoughts and feelings with compassion.

This recognition of the power of compassion to soften my grief has helped me to realize that compassion is an important component of *Pause*. Now when I observe my thoughts throughout the day, I not only stand back and observe my thoughts, I do so with the attitude of a loving parent. I notice how hard my conditioned mind is working to preserve my image and I feel gratitude for all the years of struggle it has endured, believing it needed to fight to keep me safe. At times it really did help me tremendously, but it sure tilted at a lot of windmills that didn't exist, and used up a lot of energy and well-being in the process.

TRY THIS:

1. Think of a loss. It could be of a loved one, a relationship, or even a dream that didn't come true.
2. *Pause*, breathe, let go of the tension in your body, and become aware of your surroundings.
3. Stand back and observe your thoughts and feelings about your loss as if you were a kind, loving, compassionate friend, family member, teacher or even a figure like the Dalai Lama, who exhibits so much compassion for the whole world, even to those who most people would consider his enemies.
4. As each memory arises, whether it is accompanied by sadness, guilt, regret, judgment, or even anger, be aware that you are not alone. Everyone experiences loss.
5. Watch your grief unfold as if you were observing someone else's loss.
6. Now slowly begin to pour the same empathy that you would have for someone else on your own thoughts and feelings.
7. Imagine you are an ideal parent holding a precious child with love and compassion. Only this time the child is you.

— *Time to Pause* —

I feared loss
Hovered and worried about the safety of my loved ones
Now they are gone
Primitive tears emerge from a well of despair
Allowed to flow, they cleanse me and allow
Gratitude to heal me
Grateful for the years I had with my husband, my daughter,
my dogs

I say "My"
Each of them had their own lives, made their own choices
I am blessed
One of their choices was loving me
Allowing me to love them
And we still do.

They no longer need anything from me
I need nothing from them
Our love lives on in my heart
Ego fears are laid to rest
The worst has happened

REFLECTIONS IN VERSE

These poems written at the time of Will's, Erin's, and Amber's deaths reflect the way Pause helped me to shift from the almost unbearable despair in my mind to the grief tempered by loving compassionate peace in my quiet place, which I refer to as my soul in these poems.

As you lay dying
Your body, a chrysalis
Holds the soul that wants to fly

Your love enfolds me
I shall not be alone
My soul does not know loneliness
Only my mind can feel despair

* * *

My physical mind grieves in darkness
My soul lets go in light

* * *

No one ever told me
Of the energy it takes to die
The energy required from me
To hold you as you leave.

For three days after you were gone,
Grief, confusion, exhaustion, reign
Today my soul peeks out from under the debris
Your soul, set free of personhood
Invites me now to rest.

* * *

Evening
I talk to you
Stillness answers

This morning I found you
As sunlight lit the trees
I find you in the stillness
Without the world to define your departure
You are part of the flow
Bodies are not built to last forever

Now your soul
My mate
Abides with all beings
That exist beyond the ability of minds to contain them.

So Peace beyond understanding
Is not limited
By my mind's ability to understand
In silence, my heart can understand.

* * *

Perhaps I will learn
From encounters with despair

To touch my memories
With gratitude and compassion

Heal the memories in my mind
With time

Embrace the love
That's always mine.

My observer
Like the centre of the lake
Observes the storm raging on the surface
Compassion for the boat tossed by the waves.

* * *

Your death throes were terrible
I did my loving best
To save you from them
I suffered with you

Bad enough to do that once
I do not need my mind
To enter every silence
With your pain and mine.

In this moment
Now
That suffering is over.
Celebrate our love,
As always untouched by life
And death.

* * *

My mind and body are bereft
Your warm body, loving words are gone

My soul, emboldened by your soul
Steps forward and teaches me how to live
Alone.

* * *

I grieve what is gone
Romance admiration, respect
How could I dishonour that amazing gift
By whining because you are no longer here to give me more.

You left me a legacy of wondrous memories
In the mirror of your eyes
I saw the Me I want to be
In your honour, I will not let that mirror dim.

Last night, the music laid bare
The beauty that we shared
I sobbed in utter despair
This morning I am cleaned out and rested.

*　*　*

When I am grieving
I turn to poetry.
Poets are not limited
to the mortal world
They create a path where I can find you.

Pablo Naruda said:
"...Absence is a house so vast
That inside you will pass through its walls
And hang pictures on the air"

I will always be blessed by Will's and Erin's love
It lives on in me, even as I step...
Into the vast house of their absence
And learn...
To hang pictures on the air.
Mary Oliver would have said,
"This is the earnest work"

* * *

I step up to the threshold of my life
      without Will and Erin
And look out on my path,
      cleared by years of caring for them
My mind would fill this newly empty path
      with its priorities
I *Pause*
Appoint my soul to be the chief traffic cop
As I step into the rest of my life.

My golden retriever, Amber, stayed with me as I cared for
Will and grieved for him and died a year after Will died.

The memory of Amber, lying dead on the grass
So beautiful, my heart poured tears…pain so deep
Relief began to come with loving gratitude for all the
      years of love and joy with her and Will
I can no longer touch them with my lips and hands
Yet the love I feel for them in my heart is as alive as I am.

My daughter was very ill and died a year later:

I cry from my guts
The depth of my being
My baby is gone
I am one with every animal that loses a child

I look out at the trees and know
We are only visitors to this life
Yet I am deeply connected to her soul
So grateful for all the time we had together

We shared laughter and tears for 52 years

Love and closeness beyond the bonds of family
She lives on in my heart

I don't know how I know
But I do
She's at peace.

Fresh water flowing down the river, life goes on.
Erin's ashes in a box, she's gone, she's here
Two eagles circle overhead
Tears wrenched from my guts
The river; the birds; the sun; a rock reflected in the river; a
    spider in its web
Despair; life; beauty.

After two years
The slightest reminder can still unleash my tears
They continue to cleanse me as they fall
And most of the time I am at peace
Enriched by Erin, Will and Amber
So blessed that they are such a big part of my life
Even as I move on without their physical presence.

What I need from you while I grieve

Join me in silence
If I want to talk, just listen
If there must be words, let them be of love and compassion.

If you share your experiences of grief right now
You move me from the path I must find for my own grief

If my grief rekindles your own
Please ask me for support at a different time
I will want to be there for you
As you are for me right now.

Please don't tell me how much better or worse
I will feel later
I am most at peace when I am in this moment
Now.

Only in past and future thought
Do I suffer
In this moment, I grieve.

PART V – *PAUSE* IN DAILY LIFE

— *Time to Pause* —

I Pause
Observe my thoughts
Into a tidy bundle
Until they slowly go to rest

I sigh
In silent freedom
Sometimes bliss

Thoughts
Like naughty children
Creep back out
Stir mud
Into my quiet pool of Being

Pause again
With an indulgent smile
Until thoughts crawl back
Into my ego self

Over and over we play this game
As gradually the balance shifts
Quiet centre grows stronger
Conditioned thoughts begin to take their rightful place
Keepers of knowledge, solvers of problems
Under the guidance of
My stillpoint self

Pause
One breath at a time
Living fully in the noisy world
I learn to mute the din within

To Do or Not To Do

When do I step up
And try to save the world?

When do I stand back
Send love?

Only my centre knows for sure.

Some people are meant to live in war-torn, primitive places and save the world's starving children, and some are not. Some years ago, my mentor introduced me to this concept: although we can be aware of the plight of our world and that volunteering to help is important, we may not be one of the heroic, wonderful people who are truly called from their deep, intuitive souls to live in a mud hut. I felt such a relief when I heard him.

I am definitely not excited about volunteering in rugged conditions, but I feel strongly pulled to right many of the wrongs in the world. I often see problems in areas that to others are generally accepted as okay and normal. From childhood on, I reacted to the old fable about the emperor who wore no clothes. You may recall some charlatans convinced the emperor to spend large amounts of money on the finest clothes. He believed they made the clothing for him when actually it did not exist. He was so proud of his new "clothes" that he paraded down the street, and everyone oohed and aahed about how wonderful they were, until a small child looking on from the side of the road said, "The emperor wears no clothes!" I often feel like that child. I frequently feel the compulsion to speak up, to take on the cause, to get others to see that the emperor really is naked.

This tendency has motivated me to take on many projects, such as a large voter registration drive, changing hospital policy to allow fathers to participate in the birth of their children, and allowing parents to be with their children when they are being treated in ER. I sign petitions and join marches. As I look back on my history of involvement, I realize that I feel good about some of what I did, while other times I was tilting at windmills and taking energy away from family or work. I think I was driven by a belief that if something is wrong, I should be willing to fix it. Now I know some things are not mine to fix, some are, and only my intuitive centre knows for sure.

Pause has given me a whole new way of approaching what I take on, not only in the world at large, but in relationships as well. When I *Pause*, breathe, and observe what my conditioned mind is telling me about a cause I am considering, I am able to determine whether it is something that really needs doing, and whether it is right for me to do or not. Guilt is usually not the right reason to take on a cause. It often leads to resentment later. Not doing anything can lead to helplessness and denial. The right balance can be found in our wise centre where we move beyond our conditioned thoughts.

We are inundated by more news and information about suffering than we can possibly handle and run the risk of accepting the unacceptable because of overwhelm. Political systems, likewise, seem so outrageously dysfunctional that people are accepting behavior that is antithetical to everything our culture has always stood for.

I believe we need to be awake and aware, and trust our inner wisdom to determine what we can do.

From the widest world view to issues in my neighbourhood and hometown, I find pausing the video, standing back, and observing helps me. Rather than blundering in or letting my thoughts overwhelm me with problems, it saves me from the stress I would otherwise experience. From my wise quiet centre, I know when and what would be right for me to do, and when it is right to just send love and compassion.

TRY THIS:

1. Turn on the news, and while it is on, *Pause*, breathe, and observe what your mind is saying in response to the information coming at you.
2. If you find yourself getting angry and judgmental, observe those emotions with compassion.
3. If you are telling yourself that you need to do something, observe that message objectively. You may decide to send a donation, make a phone call, sign a petition, or do something more active. Or you may just send compassionate thoughts to those who are suffering...and to those who are able to take more action.

HARMONY OF MIND AND SOUL

Look no further
For a friend

The best
Is
Deep inside

Almost everything our conditioned minds are searching for exists in our quiet centre, or soul. We don't even have to go looking for it—as soon as we stop listening to our thoughts, it is available. Our centre is able to love without judgment and defensiveness, weigh in on any problem with intuitive wisdom, and provides us with a stillness free from the stress of the world and of our own making.

The conduit between our busy mind and our quiet centre is our observer, the part of us that is able to observe our thoughts rather than listen to and believe the constant dialogue in our heads. That constant dialogue interprets the world and prevents us from experiencing it.

I am aware that there are many people who are afraid of allowing their world to become quiet, fearing what will fill the silence. Ironically that fear is manufactured by thoughts that, when observed, lose their power to frighten us.

Our minds are used to functioning without the support of our rich inner resources. When we first begin to find our inner peace, it seems like our busy minds are responsible for separating us from it, and it is tempting to see our minds and quiet centres as enemies. Even some spiritual practices and religions suggest negative attributes to the ego and set up a competition with the soul, but we need both. I think our souls and our conditioned minds can learn to work together.

Our minds are absolutely necessary to our functioning in the world. They do everything, from learning how to earn a living to knowing how to perform all the tasks of everyday life. Our minds know how to cook meals, brush teeth, find the way home, etc. They just work too hard and need training to be quiet when they are not needed. They are like a toddler who is never ready to go to bed and fights bedtime.

Our souls are not judgmental; they are like the parent or partner of our dreams, always loving and compassionate. They are also the seat of our intuitive wisdom. Through *Pause,* we find a way to quiet our minds so that we feel and know the steady presence of soul in our lives.

What a team the mind and soul make! Soul balances the activities of the mind with wisdom and compassion.

TRY THIS:

1. *Pause,* breathe, and observe your thoughts with love and compassion. That love and compassion that your observer is pouring over your thoughts comes from your quiet place or soul.
2. Notice how good that quiet place inside feels.
3. *Pause* every time you sense that you are stressed and your world seems noisy. There is a quiet place waiting for you to notice.

MY RELATIONSHIP WITH PHYSICAL PAIN

Buddhists say:
Pain is inevitable; suffering is optional

I have some chronic arthritic pain that sometimes moves in and takes over my consciousness. Everything else fades into insignificance as my thoughts surround the pain with fear, helplessness, and other negative emotions. Pain is a useful messenger saying that there is something wrong; we need to listen to it and take appropriate steps to deal with its cause. Whether we are dealing with acute pain or have done all we can to deal with the cause, *Pause* can often help us to alleviate some suffering.

When I *Pause*, breathe, and observe the pain with compassion, I can sometimes create enough emotional distance from it that the suffering of the pain eases. It's real and still there, but when I stop believing all my thoughts about it, I find some relief from the tension my thoughts were creating. Sending deep healing breaths to the pain can frequently even lessen the pain physically.

A positive side effect of observing and breathing into the pain can also be a sense that I am doing something proactive and I am not just a victim.

I will not go into great detail with this issue as there are many books written on the subject. I particularly like Jon Kabat-Zinn's book, *Full Catastrophe Living: Using the Wisdom of Your Body and Mind to Face Stress, Pain and Illness.*

TRY THIS:

1. If you get a minor pain like a paper cut on your finger or an annoying hangnail, *Pause,* observe the pain, and notice what your thoughts are telling you about it.

2. If you have chronic pain, *Pause,* breathe into it with compassion, observe what your thoughts are telling you, and try changing some of those thoughts. The act of compassion for your own discomfort often moves you out of the tension that increases your pain response.

3. Acute pain can also respond positively to your compassionate breath, and when panic gives way to calm, you may be more able to move with increased clarity to diagnose and treat the pain.

COPING IN THE MOMENT

Moments are manageable
Anticipation creates monsters
The past is full of them

During the three-and-a-half years that I cared for my husband at home, there were many opportunities to put the *Pause* exercise to work. One such opportunity was this:

One evening, the scheduling computer failed to send an aide to put my husband to bed. It was the first time in over two years this happened. As I struggled to care for him, I was grateful that my mind had not prepared a scary, dramatic scene to fit this event into. I was amazed that with a few moments to *Pause* and keep my mind from taking off into a story about it, I did okay. I was not preoccupied with my own distress about what I needed to do, which made it easier for me and allowed me to be more present with my husband. I was able to focus more on making it comfortable for him and even found some humour, which helped both of us.

As difficult as it was, anticipatory dread would have made it worse. It was a powerful lesson. When my mind has time to write a scary script about what might happen, it is much harder to deal with the actual event. Having said that, I did what I could to be sure that the computer wasn't allowed to screw up again any time soon!

There is what happens to us and there is what we tell ourselves about what happens. We can handle much more than we think we can, if we do not attach catastrophic labels to events. Events like these reinforce my determination to take time every day to remember to

Pause. The more it becomes a habit; the more readily it is available when I need it.

With practice, you can *Pause* during any situation and often create a more positive outcome. Conditioned, fearful, or defensive thoughts move aside and allow my wise Self to contribute. With practice I find that a *Pause* in the midst of just about any interaction helps to alleviate my stress, and I find it is often contagious. The person I am interacting with often unconsciously also takes time to breathe.

TRY THIS:

1. *Pause,* breathe, and relax your body.
2. Remember the last time something difficult happened that you had not anticipated.
3. Were you able to cope better than you thought you would?
4. The next time you notice your mind playing out catastrophic scenarios, *Pause.*
5. Have a chat with your mind about how these things are likely not to happen, or if they do, you now have evidence that you can cope better in the moment without predetermined negative emotions to hamper you.
6. If you do have a challenging event coming up, like a job interview, you might want to create a positive image about how it will go. See yourself handling it with calm assurance.
7. In the actual interview, if you feel yourself getting tense, take a breath and *Pause.*

THE *PAUSE* OF ACCOMPLISHMENT

How efficient are you when you are rushed, stressed, and trying to multi-task? I find the time it takes to *Pause* before I take on a task is time well spent.

When my mind is in the driver's seat pushing me to hurry through a chore, I hear, "I don't want to do this, shouldn't have to do this, don't have enough time..." The noise in my head distracts me from being present. I don't notice the dish on the edge of the counter, knock it over, and now add cleaning up the mess to what I had to do already.

Over time, *Pause* has become an integral part of my life. It helps me to show up and pay attention to the task I am doing. I am less likely to knock that dish on the floor, but if I do, it can be a wake-up call that reminds me to *Pause*. I realize at that point that I am not present and am trying to get things done without my centre. The time taken to *Pause* and get centered makes all the difference.

No matter how simple or complex the task, we need the technical expertise of our minds and the intuitive wisdom, concentration, and patience of our centre. We need the whole team. Thich Nhat Hahn was right when he suggested the importance of being fully present with each dish while doing the dishes. In the end, there is such a feeling of accomplishment, and we would have robbed ourselves of that if we had listened to an inner dialogue about wishing we were somewhere else.

When I was a caregiver for my husband, a lot of the time I went about the many tasks that filled my day with gratitude to have him at home with me and gratitude for the many workers who came to help us with such grace. But...I had my moments when I was tired, missing having lunch with a friend, or just having a day when I could do whatever I wanted to do. At times like that, a moment to *Pause* saved me. The first deep breath helped to release the tension from my body that had been building as my thoughts had been flooding my awareness with self-pity, resentment, and other unattractive emotions.

Yes, when I observed what was going on in my head, I uncovered all sorts of thoughts that I hate to have to admit to. Feeling shame for those thoughts added insult to injury. But when I observed them with compassion, I often felt like a kind friend had come along with a hug. That caring understanding came from within my own consciousness, and I learned that I could access it any time I needed it with a moment to *Pause*. The more frequently I remember to *Pause*, the more available my inner best friend becomes.

TRY THIS:

1. The next time you do a mundane task like dishes or mowing the lawn, *Pause* before you begin.
2. Be aware of what your thoughts are telling you about the task. If you find resentment, impatience, or worrying thoughts about something else, just breathe and observe those thoughts.
3. Bring your attention into the moment. Feel the water on your hands if you are doing the dishes, or feel the ground beneath your feet and the smell of nature if you are mowing the grass.
4. As you come into the moment, allow yourself to feel gratitude for the water, for the green living grass.
5. As you do the chore, keep bringing your focus back to the moment and what you are doing.

LOVING FROM STILLNESS

Love as a way of life
Happens
When I shift my focus from my ego's
Prison of fearful separation
My ego needs love
My soul is love

Pause is a pathway to knowing love as a way of life. When we stop our ego-driven lives long enough to observe what our egos believe, we begin to understand how they are running our lives. We can then find our way out of our prison of fear and separation.

When we observe our thoughts rather than automatically listening to and believing them, we begin to understand the walls of the prison that separates us from love. We recognize how hard we work to polish and protect the face we present to the world. This outer identity can separate us from love.

Our egos separate us from the world we live in. When we are lost in thoughts, we fail to see and experience the world around us. I recently moved into a retirement community, which is so different from living alone in the woods by a river. I was overwhelmed at first. As with other areas of my life, *Pause* has helped me to make this transition. I *Pause* as I walk out of the door of my apartment and notice that sometimes my thoughts are setting up barriers between me and the people I will see. They may be bringing in old fears of not being liked and accepted. When I observe those thoughts and find my quiet place, I am able to remember the title of Gerald Jampolski's book, *Love is Letting Go Of Fear*. I try to *Pause* as I walk out the door and feel calm acceptance for myself and others.

Our egos separate us from our fellow humans. We fear them when they are different. We judge them when they do things that are harmful and cruel as they listen to their egos. If we can look at others with compassion rather than judgment, they are less apt to be frightened in a way that makes them hang onto destructive behaviours even more tenaciously. It doesn't mean that we condone, but we come to a place of understanding.

Pause, breathe, and observe your thoughts. Don't try to change them or argue with them, just be with them and begin to feel the stillness. This stillness contains no fear or judgment. Fear and judgment come from thoughts, which are the output of the ego.

In order to experience real change in our lives, shifting awareness out of thought and into the quiet place inside, takes practice. That doesn't mean hours of arduous exercise or even hours on a meditation pillow. *Pause* can be done in the course of a few breaths. When my quiet place takes over, it embraces my ego with compassion, and understands that it functions with the highest motives. Believing in a fearful world, it wants to protect me. With practice, I begin to notice that when stillness moves in, fear subsides.

This is the peace that passes understanding.

TRY THIS:

1. *Pause* and as you observe your thoughts, take each one and place it with compassion and appreciation into the background.
2. Allow the quiet to move forward like a gentle mist.

PAUSE FOR FREEDOM

I am free
Unless my thoughts
Tell me I am not

Looking objectively at my life when I was caring for my husband at home, most would not have seen me basking in freedom. When my head told me my situation was dire, my feelings lined up behind the thoughts, and I felt stuck. When that happened, it was a signal that it was time to *Pause*. My chores turned into accomplishments in the absence of mind-made complaints. Outside the box of old "poor me" conditioned thoughts, I recognized that it was my choice to care for my husband at home. In that moment, I felt such gratitude for him in my life.

I have heard many stories of prisoners behind bars who use their time to create and learn. One of my favourite examples of enduring freedom of spirit while physically incarcerated is Victor Frankel. During his years in a concentration camp during World War II, he used his time to study his fellow inmates. He discovered that those who survived, like him, found meaning in spite of their horrific circumstances. Throughout his time in the camps, he wrote a book about his findings, using any scraps of paper he could find and hiding them from his captors. Shortly before the end of the war, his book was found and destroyed. When he was released, he wrote it again. His ability to bypass the defeated thoughts one might expect in such a situation provided a gift to the world in the form of his book, *Man's Search For Meaning*. They had imprisoned his body but never his soul.

Most of us reading this book are not living in a concentration camp but many feel trapped. Problems can pile up and seem insurmountable—health, money, job, family—I could go on and on. Whatever trap we feel we are in, if we try to spring it only with the mind that helped create it, we will remain prisoners of the self-created bars.

It takes another perspective to find options to freedom. When we *Pause* and quiet the thoughts of hopelessness, we will find a place of quiet. Let's take ourselves there and feel calm surround our dilemma. Don't force it; just keep breathing into centre. Deep wisdom is available that can see through what had seemed insurmountable.

In the beginning of this practice, the solutions that come when we are not listening to our thoughts can often seem like magic. After a while, we begin to trust our deep source rather than the conditioned approaches we have habitually used. I wonder if this is what it means to "think outside the box."

TRY THIS:

1. Look at whatever you feel trapped by. Breathe through your body until it is still.
2. Stand back and observe your thoughts about your trap, until they slow and become quiet.
3. Allow the loving calm wisdom of your centre to surround you. Don't force it.
4. In the absence of thoughts of fear and helplessness, fresh possibilities will emerge.
5. Whenever you feel trapped, or feel any form of helplessness, observe the thoughts that produced the

feeling and allow your breath to move your focus to your calm centre.

6. Without effort, just allow the feelings to be embraced by your centre, without judgment, and be amazed by solutions that emerge when you are not trying to make them happen.

CONCLUSION

The desire to help others navigate their rocky pathways
Prevented me from giving up on mine,
Motivated me to learn from challenge and loss.
Writing helped me to integrate the coping mechanisms that
worked.
Pause became the hero of my story.
I now step into a new chapter of my life,
An octogenarian with Pause in my pocket.

This book has been a major part of my journey through a time when life has tossed me some pretty sour lemons. It is a major part of my recipe for lemonade.

As this book ends, I hope it will help to open your life to new beginnings; for new ways to apply Pause to aspects of your life that I haven't even thought of yet and for living with the "peace that passes understanding.

AND ONE LAST "TRY THIS"

Right now in this moment before you turn the last page:

Pause; Breathe; Observe your body and mind.

Imagine you are opening a fresh chapter in your life with a new healthy relationship to your thoughts and an ever-present access to the quiet place inside.

PAUSE

ABOUT THE AUTHOR

I believe that a book is like a conversation, so you deserve to know a bit about me.

My first memory of looking for someone to help me find a quiet place inside of me came when I was a teenager and a regular member of the Anglican Church. At the end of every service, the priest gave the benediction and, as I recall, he said, "May the peace of God that passes all understanding be with us now and when we are apart." Well…I didn't feel it and am not even sure I knew what I was looking for, but the search was on.

It wasn't until I was in my mid-thirties, getting a divorce, and changing my life that I began to encounter others who were also looking for that elusive peaceful place. In my late-thirties, I was blessed to find Will, my second husband and soul mate, and he was also searching for his quiet place inside .

Having been a nurse who was always running behind because I spent too much time talking to people, I went back to school in my mid-30s and got a PhD in Clinical Psychology. It was the perfect job for me as I was able to give my full attention to one person at a time. As I look back over more than thirty years as a psychologist, I was helping people find their way out of conditioning and helping them find the way to their quiet space inside, where they would find their inner wisdom. From this place, they could make choices that would free them from listening to and believing many of the fearful, self-limiting, and even self-destructive messages their minds had been using to guide their lives.

For the last forty years, I studied and practiced Buddhism, Shamanism, the teachings of Nisargadatta, and several contemporary teachers who had interpreted many of the ancient Eastern teachings into more easily understood Western language, particularly, Eckhart Tolle, Thich Nat Hahn, Catherine Ingram, Jack Kornfield, and Jon Kabat-Zinn. I studied extensively with Lee Lyon at the Foundation for Integrative Meditation. Lee had been a teacher with Swami Muktananda and has helped me to integrate the study and experience of psychotherapy with Eastern spiritual teachings. He and I, at one point, gave a continuing education lecture on psychotherapy and spirituality for the New Mexico Psychological Association.

I have worked with people one-on-one, taught classes, and led meditation groups on how to quiet the mind and discover the quiet place inside. When I see people make this discovery, it brings me such joy. They report that being able to turn off the chatter and find the quiet, wise part of themselves is life-changing, and I know it has been for me.